A Ghost Hunter's Guide to

The Most Haunted Hotels

In America

Terrance Zepke

WHAT REVIEWERS ARE SAYING ABOUT ZEPKE'S MOST HAUNTED SERIES...

"One of the things I really like about Terrance's book is that it is such an easy read. The tidbits of history keep you turning the pages, and you also learn about the paranormal investigators, who have used a variety of paranormal investigation tools...*A Ghost Hunter's Guide To The Most Haunted Places in America* is one of those books that keeps your imagination wondering what really happened."
        -Josh Schubert, **USA Travel Magazine**

"...*A Ghost Hunter's Guide To The Most Haunted Places in America*" explores the story behind these ghost story settings all throughout the country, from theatres, old factories, asylums, homes prisons, and much more. A Ghost Hunter's Guide to The Most Haunted Places in America is a must for lovers of the paranormal in America. Highly recommended.
        -James A. Cox, **Midwest Book Review**

"...while the words "adventure travel" may conjure up images of the remote or the foreign, a new book suggests that some wild rides are much closer to home. Zepke documents the supernatural in *A Ghost Hunter's Guide to the Most Haunted Houses in America*. As she points out, "Who else but an adventurous and brave soul would dare to spend time in a haunted dwelling—and pay good money to do so?"
        –Sarah Robbins, **Publishers Weekly**

"From a lunatic asylum to a brewery, ghostly presences inhabit all these places. Complete directions and site information is provided. Even if you don't get a chance to visit each of these locations, the stories and the black-and-white photos are fascinating.
        -Marcella Gauthier, **Escapees Magazine**

"You don't have to believe in ghosts to realize that certain places in our national history are haunted with legends and spirits of long ago. Terrance Zepke grew up in South Carolina knowing the tales of colonial pirates, Civil War legends, the impact of lowcountry voodoo, and the famous residents of weathered cemeteries...places you probably best not visit at night, She's written books such as *Coastal South Carolina: Welcome to the Lowcountry, Best Ghost Tales of South Carolina, Pirates of the Carolinas*, and her latest book, *A Ghost Hunter's Guide to the Most Haunted Places in America*, investigates saloons and cemeteries, former sanitariums, and penitentiaries across America where rumors of strange phenomenon seem to have some bearing...Terrance is one of the most schooled experts on paranormal in the United States."
        –Rick Steves, ***Travel with Rick Steves***

"...From Georgia to California, Terrance writes about places that are home to a ghost or two -- and tells the horrible tales that led to these creatures remaining close to where they died. Her first chapter is about the Trans-Allegheny Lunatic Asylum in West Virginia, the place that creeped her out the most in her investigations into the paranormal -- and the one closest to where I live. It is told that many of the poor souls who died in the facility -- often from experimental treatments and procedures -- continue to roam the halls. Yawsa."
        -Teresa Flatley, ***BoomThis! Magazine***

"...Zepke herself has always loved a good ghost story and heard many as she was growing up in the Carolinas. Now she has many books recording not only the stories she loves but also the history and photos of the places named. These places have all been investigated and proven haunted by the most sophisticated modern scientific equipment such as EMF detectors, which register electrical and magnetic fields, and EVP's (Electronic Voice Phenomenon), which digitally records sounds the human ear cannot detect. Each place Zepke writes about has all the tour contact information also and many black and white photos. A fun way to plan a trip, if you aren't afraid!"

-Bonny Neely (**Top 1,000 Amazon Reviewer**)

"...a journalist by training, she [Zepke] takes you on a tour of the Trans-Allegheny Lunatic Asylum in West Virginia, the Birdcage Theatre in Arizona, and the Colonial Park Cemetery in Georgia, among a dozen other places..."

-Alan Caruba, **Bookviews.com** (National Book Critics Circle)

ISBN-10: 0985539887

ISBN-13: 978-0-9855398-8-7

Cover design by Michael Swing.

Safari Publishing

Inquiries should be addressed to: www.safaripublishing.net
For more about the author: www.terrancezepke.com

1.Ghosts. 2. Paranormal. 3. Hauntings-America. 4. American Folklore-Ghosts. 5. Ghost Investigations/Tours. 6. Haunted Hotels. I. Title.

Second Edition
Printed in the U.S.A.

Terrance Zepke

A Ghost Hunter's Guide to the Most Haunted Hotels & Inns in America

About the Author

Terrance Zepke loves ghost stories and travel. She has lived and traveled all over the world during her career as a freelance adventure travel writer. She has explored every continent and enjoyed all kinds of adventures—from dog-sledding in the Arctic to surviving an overnight stay in a very haunted lunatic asylum. Even though she has lived in exciting cities, such as Honolulu and London, she calls the Carolinas her "true home." She can't decide which state she likes best so she divides her time between North and South Carolina. She grew up in the South Carolina Lowcountry, which is what ignited her interest in ghosts. The Lowcountry is full of haunted places and tales of boo hags, hoodoo, and haints. Terrance has written numerous books on the history and folklore of the Carolinas, as well as dozens of travel guides (See the last page of this book for a list of all titles).

Introduction

This book addresses the most haunted hotels and inns across America. Unlike other haunted places that may not be accessible, all of these places are open to the public and allow you to sleep in a haunted room or at least in close proximity to ghosts.

I have traveled all over the U.S. to make sure these are truly the "most" haunted and I guarantee that they are all worth a visit or overnight stay—if you dare!

After reading this book, you'll find out what happened during Stephen King's stay at the Stanley Hotel to inspire him to write *The Shining* and why the hotel has its own resident psychic. You'll discover who Chloe was and why she may never leave Myrtles Plantation. Learn why no one has been permitted to go into Room 18 of the St. James Hotel for many years. If you're female and wanting a ghostly encounter, stay in Room 545 of the Battery Carriage House Inn and there's a good chance that the Gentleman Ghost will crawl into bed with you! You'll also learn about the history and haunting of all the places discussed in this book and different options ranging from a Halloween Ghost Dinner to a Civil War Mourning Theater held in a spooky, haunted cellar.

I hope you enjoy reading *A Ghost Hunter's*

Guide to The Most Haunted Hotels & Inns in America as much as I enjoyed researching and writing it.

For more information on other books I've written and to check out my Ghost Town or to download free ghost and travel reports, visit www.terrancezepke.com.

Also, be sure to take the fun quiz I've included at the end of the book to see if you're ready to chase these ghosts!

Terrance Zepke

Stanley Hotel

Stanley Hotel

FUN FACTS:

*Even though this was an upscale resort that catered to its affluent clientele, at one time coffee and tea were not served because the owner thought it was bad for one's health. Men were only allowed to smoke and drink alcoholic beverages in one designated area—The Pinon Room. While the owner did not believe in these indulgences, he recognized that his male patrons might not come if they could not partake in these pleasures.

*There have been many infamous visitors and guests of the hotel over the years, such as Johnny Cash, Lawrence Welk, Bob Dylan, Wayne Newton, Elliot Gould, Billy Graham, Dr. Jonas Salk (the scientist who discovered penicillin), and President Teddy Roosevelt.

*Actor Jim Carrey was supposed to stay in the hotel throughout filming of his movie, Dumb and Dumber, but that didn't happen. After checking into his room, he spent less than an hour in it before returning to the lobby and checking out. He wouldn't discuss what had happened but the staff said that he seemed scared or spooked. He didn't even collect his belongings before leaving. He sent hotel staff up to the room to retrieve his luggage.

The History

Contrary to widespread belief, F.O. Stanley did not make his fortune from the Stanley Hotel or the Stanley Steamer. F.O. Stanley and his brother, F.E., got rich by selling the patent for a photographic dry plate process machine. They sold it to Kodak for nearly a million dollars, which was a heck of a lot of money in 1904.

Stanley got into the hotel business after being diagnosed with tuberculosis in 1903. His doctors recommended he leave Massachusetts and move to Colorado where the air was pure. He and wife, Flora, ended up staying in a cabin in Estes Park. During this time, his health improved greatly.

This pleased his wife, but their primitive lodging did not. At her insistence, F.O. built a house. It can still be seen today, just west of the hotel entrance.

According to *A Concise History of the Stanley Hotel* by Ron Lasky, the most unique feature it possessed was the moveable floor. F.O. had his Stanley Steamer shipped to Colorado. He drove his car into the garage, but when he was ready to leave, he didn't want to have to back out. To avoid this, he had a "turntable-style" floor built. The floor could be spun around so that the car was headed out!

A Stanley Steamer is on display in the hotel

F.O. Stanley began construction on the hotel in 1907. It took two years to build it, which included its own power supply. F.O. Stanley built a little hydroelectric plant on the nearby Fall River. This made the Stanley Hotel the first fully functioning electric hotel in the world (although it had no central heating until 1982).

Once completed, the complex contained six buildings: main hotel, manor house, Stanley hall, carriage house, manager's house and dormitory. The sum spent on the resort is believed to be $200,000 - $500,000, which doesn't include the 140 acres of land that Stanley initially purchased. Visitors will notice that a second dorm (for employees) and a few other buildings have been added over the years.

The property has had many owners since F.O. Stanley and has been in and out of bankruptcy. Currently, the hotel is owned by Grand Heritage Hotels, which bought it for $3.1 million.

Room rates averaged $6.50 a night in the early 1900s compared to $300 a night nowadays. The Georgian-Revival style architecture chosen by Stanley was just the right look for an upscale hotel. Guests and ghosts alike enjoy the appearance and ambience of the property.

The Hauntings

The Stanley Hotel was made famous by Author Stephen King. He wrote *The Shining*, which became a bestseller and was made into a Hollywood movie. The idea for the book came to King during a brief stay at the hotel. He was suffering from writer's block and his publisher suggested he take a vacation to recharge and spark his creativity. Good advice! According to some accounts, Stephen King holed up in the hotel for five months to write this novel but that is not true. While he was inspired by his brief stay, he did not write the novel there.

For those who are not familiar with the story, a man (who was played by film legend Jack Nicholson) was hired to be caretaker of the property. The hotel closed during the winter months because it was so remote and impossible to navigate the treacherous mountain roads, so he and his wife and young son were the only people there. He was supposed to be writing a novel but ended up going crazy instead. He tried to kill his family after seeing ghosts and hearing voices.

The book was published in 1977 and made into a movie in 1980. King did not like the Hollywood version of his story. For one thing, it wasn't even shot at the hotel. It was filmed at a lodge in Oregon. Secondly, it didn't much resemble his novel by the time Hollywood was done with it. He bought the rights from the studio and produced a mini-series of "The Shining" in the late 1990s. It was filmed at the Stanley Hotel.

The hotel is the perfect backdrop for a scary story since it has lots of shadowy corners and long, dark hallways. There was only a handful of guests when I visited since it was late fall. Even though the place is not nearly as remote as once was, it is still somewhat isolated—especially in late fall and winter months when tourist season is over. Also, it gets dark outside by 5 p.m. so it is a bit gloomy and spooky in many areas of the hotel. I chose that time of year because that is around the time when Stephen King visited. But it wasn't just the dark hallways and remote mountain top location that provided the inspiration for his horror story.

According to some sources, Stephen King was exploring the hotel late one evening when he had a paranormal encounter. Reportedly, he saw a "ghost boy;" one of the spirits that haunts the place. However, I was told by management that is not true. What really happened that night is quite different from that story. Stephen King was on his way up to his room after having a drink in the bar when he ended up on the wrong floor. That's when he saw twin girls (all dressed up in matching dresses, stockings, and shiny shoes) sitting on the couch. As he was thinking how odd that was, they disappeared!

The Stanley Hotel is haunted by many ghosts. Former landowner Lord Dunraven is sometimes seen in the window of Room 401. A building inspector claims to have seen a man going into a closet as he entered the room, but when he opened the closet door the man had vanished. The sounds of banging and thumping have been heard in the closet but no one is ever found when the noise is investigated.

Reportedly, Lord Dunraven scammed quite a few locals out of their money and land in his determination to build a fine hunting lodge. But he nixed his plans after Stanley offered him top dollar for the acreage.

Perhaps he's still up to his dirty tricks. From time to time, guests have complained of items missing from their room. One man swears that he put a ring on the nightstand when he went to bed and that it was gone in the morning. Yet no one—at least no human being— entered into his room during that time. Dunraven's presence is also revealed by the distinct smell of his cherry tobacco and his penchant for moving objects. He almost can't resist moving reading glasses left on a bedside table and is believed to be responsible for turning lights on and off in Room 401. Guests swear they hear footsteps outside their door but when they open the door, no one is in the hall.

F.O. and Flora Stanley

The spirit of F.O. Stanley has been spotted in the lobby, kitchen, billiards room, and the bar. Perhaps now that he is deceased he figures there is no harm in his imbibing! The spirit of his wife, Flora, is here too. She was a great fan of music and often entertained guests by playing her grand piano. Her ghost has been seen in the ballroom and piano music is heard in the music room.

However, the music abruptly stops when someone enters the room to investigate and no one is found in the room.

Remarkably, ALL of the rooms in the hotel have stories of paranormal activity. These include the bed shaking, objects being moved, inexplicable sounds, and lights being turned on and off. The most activity has been reported in Rooms 401, 407, 412, 418, and 217. In fact, Room 412 has been dubbed the "poltergeist room" because the ghost has levitated the bed on occasion. One female guest became so hysterical after it happened to her that she woke up half the hotel and the police were called to deal with the panic-stricken woman.

Room 428 is home to a cowboy ghost, which has been seen by men and women. But it seems that this spirit prefers women as it has been known to kiss a female guest before disappearing into the ether.

Even the hallway of the fourth floor is spooky. Guests and employees have reported the sounds of children running and playing and laughing. According to staff, one of the maids let her children play while she cleaned that floor. They think maybe they still like to play here. Some guests swear an unseen presence has "tucked them in" at night. The well-to-do often traveled with nannies and it is believed that the spirits of these nannies are still hard at work. Many visitors and staff have seen the spirit of a bartender, ghost boy, twin girls, and a housekeeper.

Elizabeth Wilson was the head housekeeper for the hotel when it first opened. Her story is a sad one indeed. There was a terrible storm on the night of June 25, 1911. It knocked out the power. Ms. Wilson was in charge of lighting the back-up acetylene lanterns. She was lighting a lantern in Room 217. There was a horrific explosion during this process, which resulted in the floor being destroyed and the housekeeper dropping into the room below. Thankfully, the only serious injury she incurred was two broken ankles.

Since that time, guests have reported their belongings being unpacked, their rooms being tidied, and other housekeeping services that none of the staff claimed to have done. It is believed that the housekeeper is still making sure that guests are well taken care of. When Stephen King came to the hotel, he and his wife checked in, brought their luggage upstairs, and then left for about forty-five minutes or so. When they returned, they found their belongings unpacked and the luggage stacked in the closet. When questioned, no one in housekeeping admitted to being in his room—let alone unpacking his suitcases!

But it is not just the hotel that is haunted. There has been paranormal activity reported in the Manor House, Concert Hall, and Carriage House. A homeless woman froze to death while squatting in the Concert Hall. Some believe her spirit is still here because screaming has been heard coming from the audio room when no one is in there and noises have been heard backstage.

There is a passageway in the basement that employees used to go back and forth to the hotel. It is supposed to be haunted by the spirit of a twelve-year-old girl named Katie. She was an orphan who kept warm in the winter months by hiding in the basement next to the furnace. Management kicked her out when they discovered she was living in the basement. Some believe that the spirit that lingers in the basement is this girl, but others speculate that it is haunted by the spirit of the employee who died during a cave-in that occurred in the basement many years ago.

The most haunted area of the property outside of the hotel is the Carriage House. This is where the vehicles were stored and repaired. It served as a motel in the 1970s and has been storage space ever since. There has been talk of tearing it down, which must upset its resident ghosts. Whenever anyone unlocks it and goes inside, paranormal activity occurs, such as the smell of cigar smoke when no one is smoking and the unshakable feeling of an unseen presence. One employee was knocked to the ground while she was in the old building cataloging its contents. The place is full of old objects from the hotel, including mattresses. There have been several deaths on the property over the years. When a guest dies in bed, the bed is removed and stored in the Carriage House. Perhaps some of these spirits linger here?

Several ghost groups have investigated the property and all have left with lots of EVPs and other data that support the belief that it is haunted. SyFy's Ghost Hunters have officially declared it "haunted."

With all these ghosts and paranormal activity, it is no wonder that the hotel has its own resident psychic, 'Madame Vera'.

Visitor Information

333 Wonderview Avenue

Estes Park, CO 80517

The property has been listed on the National Register of Historic Places since 1977. The 35-acre resort is also a National Historic District, including Fall River Power Plant (The resort was originally 140 acres but more than 100 acres have been sold over the years).

There are a variety of ways to explore this unique property. Ghost tours are open to the general public or you can also opt to spend the night and wait for the ghosts to come to you! Be advised that tours often sell out, so advance reservations are highly recommended. No babies or children under the age of five are permitted on tours. Special events are held seasonally, such as 'The Shining Ball'.

In addition to possible paranormal activity, guests are guaranteed spectacular panoramic views of the Rockies.

A visit to the nearby Rocky Mountain National Park is a must for hotel guests and visitors. The Rocky Mountains are among the highest elevations in America. The hotel is 7,500 feet above Estes Park.

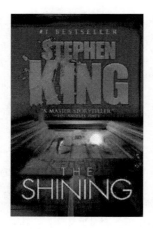

Estes Park is an hour's drive from Denver (65 miles); 16 hours from Milwaukee, Wisconsin (1,062 miles); 7 hours from Santa Fe, New Mexico (425 miles); and 12 hours from Las Vegas, Nevada (797 miles).

www.stanleyhotel.com

Myrtles Plantation

Myrtles Plantation

FUN FACTS:

When part of the television miniseries, Long Hot Summer, starring Jason Robards, Don Johnson, and Cybil Shepherd, filmed at Myrtles the cast and crew witnessed many eerie events. One morning the crew set up the game room and dining room for taping. By the time they were ready to shoot, the props had all been moved. Furniture that had been carefully placed for the scene was now back in its original location. The area had been cordoned off so there was no rational explanation. This was just the first of many unexplainable things that occurred during the taping. The cast and crew admitted they were glad when the taping was done and they could leave.

The place is believed to be haunted by the ghost of a girl named Chloe who is still seeking retribution for what was done to her.

Lots of paranormal activity has been documented including handprints that appear mysteriously on the wall mirror.

The History

This story begins with a man named David Bradford, who married Elizabeth Porter in 1785. When the couple began having children, they needed a bigger house. They built an edifice that doubled as a home and law office for David Bradford.

Things went well for the Bradford family until David got involved in the Whiskey Rebellion. Farmers used excess grain and corn to make whiskey to subsidize their income. The government began taxing it in 1791. Farmers throughout Pennsylvania protested the new tax. One of the men who joined the protest was General David "Whiskey Dave" Bradford.

When President Washington sent militia to Pennsylvania to squash the rebellion, Bradford decided it was in his best interest to leave. He fled, ending up in Louisiana, after making a brief stop in Pittsburgh to settle his family. He parted company with them for their own safety since he was a wanted man on the lamb from the law.

Around 1796, Bradford bought 600 acres of land and built an eight-room house he called "Laurel Grove." In 1799, he received a pardon for his participation in the Whiskey Rebellion from the new President John Adams. He immediately retrieved his wife and five kids from Pittsburgh and returned to Louisiana, where he lived a quiet existence until his death. All of his children, except Sarah, died of yellow fever. The former lawyer mentored law students, including a young man named Clark Woodrooff. Woodrooff fell in love with Sarah. The pair got married on November 19, 1817.

When David Bradford died, the house was left to his wife, Elizabeth. Clark and Sarah Woodrooff helped take care of the property. It was a big responsibility considering the size and scope of the plantation. It was 650 acres and much of that land was producing the highly sought after cotton and indigo crops.

Sarah and Clark had three children, who were cared for by a slave girl named Chloe. Eventually, Clark Woodruff bought the plantation from his mother-in-law, Elizabeth, although she continued to live there until her death in 1830. As his law practice grew, he found it difficult to meet the incessant demands that are part of running a big plantation. He preferred law to farming, so he hired an overseer and devoted his full attention to pursuing his legal career. His hard work paid off. He was appointed as a judge.

On January 1, 1834, he sold Laurel Grove to Ruffin Stirling. Clark lived in New Orleans for a few years before moving in with his daughter, Mary Octavia, and her husband, Colonel Lorenzo Besancon on their plantation. They lived just north of New Orleans. Clark also changed his last name from Woodrooff to Woodruff.

Ruffin Stirling and his wife, Mary, made major renovations to the property and changed the name to "The Myrtles." They traveled to Europe to find just the right furnishings for their home, which had doubled in size due to their remodeling. Just four years after finishing the extensive renovations, Ruffin died of consumption, more commonly known nowadays as tuberculosis. Despite the Civil War and many hardships, his widow stayed in the home until her death in 1880.

Mary gave the property to her daughter, Sarah, and husband, William Winter. It was devastating when the home was lost to bankruptcy just a few years later. In an odd twist of events, Sarah found the resources to buy back the plantation just two years later. William and Sarah and Mary returned to their beloved home.

William Winter was mysteriously shot in January 1871. A man on horseback approached the house. He called out William's name. William heard the summons and went outside. As soon as he stepped out, the man on horseback shot him. The killer rode away immediately after the fatal shooting. Sarah never got over her husband's death but continued to live at The Myrtles until she died in 1878. Mary Stirling died two years later at the age of 44.

The home then came under the ownership of one of her sons, Stephen Stirling. Reports vary as to whether Stephen lost the property during a card game or whether he just went bankrupt. Whatever the case, the house had several owners over the next several decades until the 1950s when it was bought by Marjorie Munson. This is when the ghostly presence was finally reported.

The Hauntings

Over the years, there have been reports of footsteps on the stairs, mysterious smells (including the smell of gunfire), objects that have been moved, handprints that appear in a mirror, ghostly sightings, and more.

Legend has it that there have been ten murders on the property, but only one is documented. That is the shooting of William Winter. So were there others or is this part of the story pure fiction? We may never know for certain given that the house is well over 200 years old and has had dozens of owners.

The most famous ghost at Myrtles is Chloe. Chloe was a slave who had an affair with Clark Woodruff. The affair allegedly began while Sarah Woodruff was laid up in bed during her third pregnancy. After the child was born and marital relations resumed (or Clark found another mistress), Clark ended the affair. Chloe feared that she would be sent to work in the fields now that the affair was over. She began spying on the family, hoping to learn some useful information.

Instead, Clark caught the young girl and was furious with her behavior. He had one of her ears cut off to show her what happens to eavesdroppers. Chloe was forced to wear a green turban forevermore to hide the deformity. This is when Chloe came up with a devious plan. She decided to poison the Woodruff family. It is unclear whether she meant for them to die or just get very sick so that she could nurse them back to health, thereby proving her value and securing her job. Chloe added ground up oleander flowers to the cake batter. Oleander is toxic when ingested.

The cake was a birthday cake for one of Clark's daughters. Chloe figured that everyone in the family would eat a slice of birthday cake. Regardless of her intent, by the end of the day, three members of the family were dead. Sarah and two of her children died within hours of eating the cake. Ironically, the person she despised the most, Clark Woodruff, didn't eat any cake.

Another slave discovered what Chloe had done and told some of the other slaves. They were fearful that the poisoning would be discovered and the wrong person blamed. During the night, the group of slaves came for Chloe. They dragged her outside and hanged her. Later, they disposed of the body in the nearby river.

Many believe that her angry spirit still haunts Myrtles, seeking retribution. Some believe these events never transpired, thereby making it impossible for

Chloe to haunt Myrtles Plantation. According to some, Sarah and the children died of yellow fever.

Marjorie Munson bought the property in the 1950s. She was disturbed by all the strange goings-on, including the sightings of a ghostly apparition. She swore she saw a ghost wearing a green bonnet on several occasions. That's when she learned the story about Chloe and her green turban.

The only thing we know for certain is that there does seem to be paranormal activity at Myrtles. Ghostly handprint images often turn up in developed photos taken by visitors of a hall mirror. And the sightings of the apparition in a green bonnet may be a former occupant and have nothing to do with Chloe. That is entirely possible given that the residence seems to be haunted by several different spirits (some believe as many as twelve ghosts), including children who have been seen playing and young girl in a long white dress. The piano often plays the same song even though no one is ever found playing it. Footsteps are sometimes heard on the stairwell but no one is there.

The spirits of Chloe, Sara, James, and Cornelia have been seen in the large mirror that once hung in the dining room. It now hangs in the hallway. Some argue that there is no record of Chloe so this story is just that—a story. But slave records were often incomplete and inaccurate. Some say the mirror was not even the same one from that era.

Strange things happened while a movie was shot at the Myrtles. During the filming of the movie, The Long Hot Summer (starring Don Johnson, Ava Gardner, Cybill Shepherd, and Jason Robards), the crew encountered paranormal activity. At the end of the day they moved furniture for a scene that was to be shot the next morning. When they arrived to shoot the scene they found that all the furniture had been moved back to its original location. The place had been secured for the shoot so this baffled all involved. They restaged the room but before they could shoot the scene they discovered the furniture had been moved again. This happened several times before they were finally able to guard the room and shoot the scene!

A guard once watched a young woman in an old-fashioned white dress walk through the gate and up to the house. She did not acknowledge him. He chased after her only to watch her "walk" right through the front door! He was so shaken by this event that he quit his job and never went near the house again.

We may never know for sure who haunts the Myrtles Plantation, but there is no doubt that it is one of the most haunted inns in our country.

Visitor Information

7747 US Hwy 61

St. Francisville, LA 70775 (22 miles north of Baton Rouge Airport)

Today, the old plantation is listed on the National Register of Historic Places and is a bed and breakfast establishment. History and mystery tours are offered. There are guest rooms in the plantation house and elsewhere on the grounds. There is also a restaurant that is open every day except Tuesdays.

www.myrtlesplantation.com

St. Francisville is 4.5 hours from Houston, TX (299 miles); 9 hours from Nashville, TN (570 miles); and 18 hours from Detroit, Michigan (1,115 miles).

Terrance Zepke

Lizzie Borden House B & B

Lizzie Borden House B & B

FUN FACTS:

This story inspired a popular rhyme:

> Lizzie Borden took an axe
> And gave her mother forty whacks.
> When she saw what she had done
> She gave her father forty-one.

In reality, her stepmother suffered 18 or 19 blows while her father was struck 11 times.

This remains one of the greatest unsolved mysteries.

The History

This is a complicated story due to all the people involved. For that reason, I am including a list of people:

Andrew Borden: father and murder victim

Abby Borden: stepmother and murder victim

Lizzie Borden: daughter and prime suspect

Emma Borden: daughter and older sister to Lizzie

Bridget Sullivan: family maid
Note: Lizzie and Emma often called her "Maggie" because that was the name of the previous maid but it is unclear if they did this as an insult or because they couldn't be bothered to remember her name

Prosecutors: Frank Moody and Hosea Knowlton

Defense attorneys: George Robinson and Andrew Jennings

John Morse: Emma and Lizzie's uncle

Adelaide Churchill: neighbor

Dr. Bowen: neighbor and family friend

Dr. Dolan: county medical examiner

Alice Russell: Lizzie's friend and witness

Eli Bence: clerk at Smith's Drug Store (where Lizzie allegedly tried to buy poison)

In addition to the cast of characters, here is a helpful timeline:

August 4, 1892. The maid, Bridget, awoke first and fixed breakfast.

Andrew Borden and his wife, Abby, had breakfast before he left for work around 9 a.m. The couple had been sick so Abby returned to the guest bedroom to lie down. Since the couple had both been sick and vomiting for the last day or two, they slept in separate rooms so as not to disturb the other.

Andrew, not feeling well, returned home around 10.45 a.m. and went into the sitting room to lie down.

Bridget had been cleaning windows until mid-morning. At that time, she returned to her room on the third floor to rest. Or so she told the police. It seems strange behavior for a young maid to go to bed mid-morning, but seeing as she may have been suffering from the same flu or stomach virus as her employers, it is plausible.

Emma was away at a friend's house.

Lizzie slept late as she also had suffered from the same flu or stomach virus as her father and stepmother. When she got up, she claimed she went out to the barn.

John Morse was visiting but he had left early that morning to visit a nephew.

At 11.15 or so, Lizzie cried out for Bridget to come. She announced that her father was dead. Shortly afterwards, Bridget discovered that Abby Borden had also been murdered.

Lizzie Borden

Lizzie told Bridget to go get Dr. Bowen, who lived across the street. Neighbors began arriving to find out what was going on after hearing all the commotion. The police were summoned. When Lizzie was questioned as to her whereabouts, she said that she had gone out to the barn. When she returned to the house she found her father.

Dr. Bowen determined that both victims had been cut and struck with a sharp object, mostly likely an ax. It was obvious that Andrew Borden had been attacked from above and behind as he slept. One eye had even been cut in half and his nose severed.

Because it was such a savage attack, the authorities did not believe that Lizzie was capable of such a thing. They didn't think it possible that a woman could do something so horrible. Unfortunately, by the time the police arrived, the crime scene had been destroyed by well-meaning neighbors and curiosity-seekers. Since there had been some concern that the family had been poisoned rather than having the flu, stomach contents were analyzed. Nothing out of the ordinary was discovered.

There was lots of contradictory evidence, such as a bloody hatchet found in a nearby farm but the blood was found to be from a chicken, not a human being. A drugstore clerk, Eli Bence, swore that Lizzie tried to buy poison from him. He refused to sell it to her because she didn't have a prescription. Lizzie denied even being in the drugstore on that day.

There were plenty of suspects to go around. At first, the investigation focused on the young maid. Then there was discussion that the uncle did it. Some thought Emma had said that she was going out of town but that she sneaked home to commit the murders. Some believe she and her sister may have planned it together. A few thought that a homicidal madman was on the loose because there had been another gruesome murder in the area shortly after the Bordens were murdered.

But many folks believed that Lizzie was the murderer. She had the means and opportunity, not to mention motive. It was well-known that she despised her stepmother. In fact, she and Emma no longer dined with their father and his new wife. Lizzie and Emma were also concerned about their inheritance because their father was spending a lot keeping up Abby's family. But he was not so generous with his daughters. He recently reduced their allowance, creating more resentment.

However, the most damaging testimony was given by Lizzie's friend, Alice Russell. She told authorities that she had discovered Lizzie in the kitchen burning a dress in the stove. This was the same dress she had worn on the day of the murders, the one that authorities had asked her to turn over to them. Lizzie had told the police that she had thrown the dress away but later changed her story. She said that there were paint stains all over the dress so she had destroyed it since she could no longer wear it.

The grand jury found sufficient cause for a trial. Lizzie Borden's criminal trial began on June 5, 1893. The fourteen-day trial was headline news across America. Roughly three dozen reporters from all the major publications were in the courtroom throughout the trial.

The prosecutor pointed out that Lizzie was angry with her father for marrying Abby Gray and for not being more indulgent with his daughters. He argued that she was afraid that he was going to leave the bulk of his estate to their stepmother. He portrayed Lizzie as selfish, greedy, and unfeeling, although he had no real proof to support his accusations.

The jury found Lizzie "not guilty." Her behavior after the trial made many in the community wonder whether the jury had made the right choice. Less than five weeks after the trial was over, Lizzie and Emma bought a thirteen-room mansion in the best part of town known as "Hill" neighborhood. They lived well, hiring live-in maids, a housekeeper, and a coachman.

But given that their childhood home didn't even have indoor plumbing in most of the house and was in one of the worst areas of town it is not surprising that they moved. Even though he had plenty of money, Andrew Borden chose to live in this rundown neighborhood because it was near most of his commercial properties, including the textile mill and bank.

Lizzie began calling herself "Lizbeth" and began associating with an actress named Nance O'Neil. They were so close that some speculated they were much more than friends. During this time, she had a falling out with her sister and they never spoke again. In fact, Emma moved away and never returned to Fall River. She believe the Emma discovered that Lizzie had been responsible for the murders and wanted nothing more to do with her sister. Or perhaps she just didn't approve of her lifestyle?

In addition to her questionable relationship with Nance O'Neil, Lizzie often threw wild parties and carelessly spent money. Despite her wealth, Lizzie was caught stealing a couple of paintings worth less than $100. The store didn't press charges and the matter was handled discreetly. This incident does show that Lizzie was capable of committing a crime and may have even enjoyed the thrill of doing something dangerous and illegal since there was no good reason why she stole the cheap artwork.

Or perhaps she just had some mental issues?

Who killed Mr. and Mrs. Borden and why they were murdered remains an unsolved mystery. Lizzie remains a good suspect, especially given her behavior after the murders. It supports the theory that she suffered from a mental disorder, such as being bi-polar or having a split personality ("Lizbeth"). There is no proof that her father abused her or her sister, but if he did it could explain the brutal murders.

It is unlikely that Bridget committed the murders, but she may have known more than she told the police. She moved far away as soon as the trial was over and never returned. She didn't work for Lizzie or Emma—not even for one day. One popular theory is that she was paid off by Lizzie (or by Lizzie and Emma) to keep quiet.

Some believe that a young man named William, who was Andrew's illegitimate son, was the culprit. He tried to extort money from his father. When that failed, he killed him and Abby in a fit of anger. He may have believed that he was in the will and would inherit a portion of the estate.

Some conspiracy theorists even allude to a conspiracy between Uncle John, Lizzie, Emma, Bridget, and Dr. Bowen.

The family was reunited in death. Emma and Lizzie were buried alongside their father and stepmother and mother in the family burial plot at Oak Grove Cemetery. Emma eventually died from a fall down some steps while Lizzie died from pneumonia on June 1, 1927 at the age of 66.

The Hauntings

The property is now owned by LeAnn Wilbur, who has reported a great deal of paranormal activity. Since two brutal (and unsolved) murders and so much unhappiness transpired here, it is no wonder this is one of the most haunted places in America.

Wilbur has felt pressure and a "heaviness" in the bedroom where Mrs. Borden was murdered. She awakened when she began having trouble breathing. She felt like someone was hitting her in the chest. Finally, she collapsed onto the floor where she lay for a long time succumbing to a feeling of great sorrow. This bizarre incident spooked her so much that she never spent another night in that room.

The SyFy television show, Dead Files, brought in psychics to investigate. They all have sensed an intense energy that they are sure is an angry female spirit. One psychic sees Lizzie as having a split personality. Some have become nauseas and become plagued with a weird feeling that led to being really stressed by the situation. They have heard heavy breathing and growling. One picked up on rape and incest while another saw a man striking a woman. Was this Mr. Borden? Did he abuse his daughters? Did they kill him?

While these questions will probably remain unanswered, we do know where the hauntings take place. In addition to Mrs. Borden's bedroom, a great deal of paranormal activity has been reported in the sitting room where Mr. Borden was killed, as well as in the cellar.

Guests have reported strange incidents and many have been touched by an unseen presence during the night. Some have seen what they describe as a large shadow or black mass in their room. A night manager saw a large shadowy shape in the doorway and watched it disappear into the wall. The manager has seen this same figure on several other occasions. Since Mr. Borden was nearly 6' tall, many believe it is his ghost that appears late at night.

Several guests have claimed to have seen a young woman in Victorian clothing dusting furniture and smoothing or straightening the bed covers. Even those who have not seen anything strange have reported their beds messed up and luggage disturbed. Some guests have complained of hearing footsteps during the night going up and down the stairs, walking overhead, and hearing muffled conversations, even when they are the only guests currently staying at the inn.

During an investigation conducted by Travel Channel's Ghost Adventures, a nightstand drawer opened on its own and a flashlight turned on by itself. They had a séance and an EVP recorded "tell 'em about the girl!"

Bedroom in Lizzie Borden B & B

Visitor Information

230 2nd Street
Fall River, Massachusetts 02721
www.lizzie-borden.com

The Lizzie Borden House is now the Lizzie Borden Bed and Breakfast Museum. Visitors can tour the house, which is open seven days a week, except on holidays. Adventurous souls can spent the night in a room, rent a floor of the house, or book the entire house for an overnight stay or investigation.

Visit this link if you'd like to see their ghost cams, https://lizzie-borden.com/index.php/ghost-cams.

Fall River is 50 miles south of Boston (near Providence, RI); 5 hours from Trenton, NJ (252 miles); and 10 hours from Richmond, VA (570 miles).

Terrance Zepke

Chateau Marmont

Chateau Marmont

FUN FACTS:

The structure was the first property in Los Angeles that was built to be earthquake resistant.

More affairs and convalescence from cosmetic surgery has occurred here than probably anywhere else in "Tinsel Town."

It is decorated with fine antiques that had belonged to some of America's finest families for generations before being sold for pennies on the dollar during the Great Depression.

The History

Everyone's heard the saying "What happens in Vegas, stays in Vegas." The same could be said about Chateau Marmont. Discretion is drilled into each and every single employee.

Former President and Founder of Columbia Pictures, Harry Gohn, summed it up best, "If you must get into trouble, do it a Chateau Marmont." It is probably the most famous hideaway in Hollywood.

The property was designed to mimic Chateau d'Amboise in the Loire Valley. Fred Horowitz saw Chateau d'Amboise while on a trip to France. He came home with lots of photos of the royal estate. He showed them to European-trained architect, Arnold Weitzman. Horowitz told the architect that he wanted an apartment complex designed to look like the French chateau. Weitzman came up with a seven-story, L-shaped building based on the photos and his discussions with Horowitz.

Since the property was located on Marmont Lane and was built to look like a French chateau, the name Chateau Marmont was conceived. It took two years to build because the place was designed to be earthquake resistant. Reportedly, this was the first earthquake proof property built in Los Angeles. The deluxe apartment complex was completed on February 1, 1929. The architect and contractor did their jobs well given that the Chateau Marmont has withstood many earthquakes, including significant ones in 1906, 1952, 1971, 1989, and 1994.

During the Great Depression, Horowitz sold the property to Al Smith for $750,000. Smith converted it into a hotel with sixty-three guest rooms. He added nine Spanish-style cottages and four bungalows and filled the place with antiques he acquired from depression-era estate sales.

Even today, many of those same antique candelabras, oversized mirrors, velvet couches, statutes, and plush oriental rugs remain throughout the hotel.

Guests are sleeping in the same rooms and sharing the same views as F. Scott Fitzgerald, Greta Garbo, Jean Harlow, Dustin Hoffman, John Belushi, Marilyn Monroe, Clark Gable, Charlie Chaplin, Boris Karloff, Howard Hughes (wouldn't leave his penthouse suite but did stand on his balcony with binoculars to check out the action at the pool), Jim Morrison, John Lennon, Helmut Newton, and Led Zeppelin. In fact, Greta Garbo lived at the Marmont for a while and members of the rock band, Led Zeppelin, reportedly rode motorcycles through the lobby. Guests may feel as though they have time warped into a bygone era until they step onto their private terraces and balconies, which overlook Sunset Boulevard.

The hotel became a Historical Landmark in 1976.

The Hauntings

How did it go from being a celebrity hideaway to one of the most haunted hotels in America? The two go hand in hand given that it is reportedly haunted by Howard Hughes, Marilyn Monroe, and John Belushi Some believe that the spirits of Boris Karloff and Jim Morrison linger here.

According to one legend, the place is cursed. Many who have stayed have suffered tragedy or death soon thereafter. It was shortly after her honeymoon here that Sharon Tate was murdered. Natalie Wood had a premonition that she would die in the water while staying at Chateau Marmont. Reportedly, the seventeen-year-old actress came to the hotel often while having an affair with her *Rebel Without A Cause* director, Nick Ray. Helmut Newton had a fatal car crash right after leaving the Marmont. Jim Morrison jumped off the roof and F. Scott Fitzgerald had a heart attack after walking across the street to buy cigarettes.

The biggest scandal attached to the Marmont was the death of Comedian and Actor John Belushi. He overdosed on March 5, 1982 after consuming a lethal combination of cocaine, heroin, and liquor. He had been partying with friends and colleagues, including Robert DeNiro and Robin Williams.

After hanging out at "On The Rox" all night, Belushi invited the group to keep partying at his bungalow at the Marmont. Belushi kept partying long after everyone else had gone home. His manager found the 33-year-old actor dead on the floor of Bungalow #3.

John Belushi

Ever since that time, guests have seen his spirit in the bungalow and on the grounds. A family once lived there for a year while there house was undergoing renovations. The little boy was often heard laughing and carrying on as if he was playing with someone. When a family member went into the room to check on him, they found the child alone. When asked why he was laughing, the boy says the "funny man" kept making him laugh. Later, the family learned the story about John Belushi and came to believe that he was the "funny man." When the mother showed her son a picture of Belushi in a book, he started yelling, "That's the funny man! That's my friend!"

Over the years, many guests have claimed to feel

an unseen presence in Bungalow #3. Throughout the property, guests and former employees (current employees are not permitted to speak about anything that happens there) have reported lots of strange things, such as windows opening on their own, small and large objects being moved, muffled voices and laughter, and ghostly sightings. Some have said that they have seen floating heads and shadowy figures in bed with them. If they get up and turn the lights on, the apparition disappears.

Of course, it is hard to verify any of this given that the hotel does not permit ghost investigations.

Visitor Information

Always protective of patrons' privacy, no one is permitted inside the hotel unless he is a paying guest. If you are a registered guest, you may explore all you like —if you can afford the nightly rates. But even paying guests are not allowed to conduct official investigations.

Note: The Bar Marmont is down the street from the hotel and is open to the public. It offers the same classic ambience and celebrity gawking, but without the ghosts.

8221 Sunset Boulevard

Hollywood, CA 90046

www.chateaumarmont.com

Los Angeles/Hollywood is 960 miles from Portland, OR; 2 hours from San Diego, CA (130 miles); and 15 hours from Denver, CO (1,020 miles).

FYI: While you're in the area, you may want to check out another haunted hotel. Named after Theodore Roosevelt, the **Roosevelt Hotel** opened on May, 15, 1927. It was financed by Hollywood executives and celebrities, including Louis B. Mayer, Mary Pickford, and Douglas Fairbanks. The first Academy Awards ceremony was held here. It lasted only fifteen minutes! Every time a star is added to the Hollywood Walk of Fame, a party is held at the hotel afterwards. This is because the famous walkway is right outside the hotel.

It is reportedly haunted by Marilyn Monroe and Montgomery Clift. The most haunted area is the 9th floor near Room 928 where the actor stayed while making *From Here To Eternity*. Footsteps and a bugle playing have been heard. Many feel this is Montgomery Clift, who paced the hallway outside his room while learning his lines and practicing the bugle his character played in the movie.

Another haunted area is Cabana 246 where Marilyn Monroe lived for a while. Guests and employees have seen ghostly images of Marilyn while looking in a mirror in that cabana. Even though the mirror was owned by Marilyn, she left it behind when she moved out of the hotel. The cabana is available but the mirror was removed a long time ago.

Guests have also complained of cold spots in the Blossom Room, unexplainable noises, shadowy figures, and phones lifting off the hook.

7000 Hollywood Boulevard. Los Angeles, CA 90028. www.thompsonhotels.com/hotels/la/hollywood-roosevelt

Battery Carriage House Inn

Battery Carriage House Inn

FUN FACTS:

Guests can book the inn's **Ghost Adventure Package**...if they dare!

This neoclassical landmark is located at the southern part of the peninsula at Battery Park, which was originally established as a fort. It was converted into a park in 1837 but used as an artillery battery during the Civil War. That's why you'll see so many monuments, memorials, cannons, and other wartime artifacts throughout the park.

The inn has TWO ghosts and one is headless!

The History

Founded in 1670 and originally named Charles Town after King Charles II, the port city has seen a lot over the years. The first shot of the Civil War was fired from here. Many other "firsts" took place here, such as our nation's first successful submarine attack, America's first golf course, and first theatre, Dock Street Theatre. Since Charleston is one of the oldest and most haunted cities in America, it is hard to pinpoint the "most" haunted place. That said, I think one of the most haunted places in this historical port city is the Battery Carriage House.

During the summer of 1843, Samuel Stevens bought the neoclassical-style property for $4,500. It was designed so that the length of the house faced the sea rather than the road. This was typically done so as to maximize ocean breezes during the long, hot summer. This is also the reason why porches were built to run the length of a house. Large windows opened onto these covered porches, allowing for greater ventilation.

This was used as a summer home for the Stevens family for sixteen years until it was sold to John Blacklock. Blacklock had lived on prestigious Bull

Street before moving to this house on the Battery. He was forced to vacate during the Civil War's Siege of Charleston. Like much of Charleston, the house suffered damage during this assault. Most likely, Blacklock lacked the money to repair the house. Most southerners were hard hit by the war. This is when many Yankees came in and bought distressed properties at bargain basement prices.

Blacklock sold the house to Colonel Lathers in 1870. While Lathers hailed from Georgetown, he had been a colonel for the Union army. He married a wealthy New York woman, whose family was in the banking business. He was also a factor, which meant that he arranged the sale and transport of cotton for local planters to Northern cotton mills.

Lathers hired renowned Charleston architect John Henry Devereaux to complete the extensive renovations. A library and new ballroom were added. Although it was called a ballroom, it was meant to be a meeting room. Reportedly, Lathers used the room to bring southern businessmen and legislators together with Northern bankers and legislators in the hopes of reviving South Carolina's economy.

Despite his best efforts, South Carolinians were not receptive to working with Yankees to rebuild the state. Eventually, Lathers left Charleston. He sold the house to Andrew Simonds in 1874. He is the great-great grandfather of the current owner. Simonds was the founder of the First National Bank of South Carolina. He was also a businessman. He started Imperial Fertilizer Company. Nearly bankrupt plantation owners could hold onto their homes by supplying phosphate, which is used to make fertilizer. Simonds expanded his empire to include a fleet of trading ships. Sadly, his oldest son and namesake, Andrew Simonds Jr. was a troubled young man. He became a drunk and a bum. He ended up in a Baltimore sanatorium.

Andrew and Daisy Simonds lived on Battery Park for more than forty-five years. They were quite happy and often threw grand parties. There is a great story about Daisy climbing up onto the roof of the ballroom one night. Presumably, this was during one of their wild parties. She fell through the glass skylight and would have been killed, if she hadn't miraculously fallen right into one of the large chandeliers.

In the early 1920s, it was owned by a couple who converted part of the property into a cheap motor lodge or court. Since their last name was Pringle, they called it "Pringle Court." By the 1940s, Charleston had become a military town filled with Navy sailors. Nightclubs and bars sprang up all along the waterfront. Rooms at Pringle Court were rented out by the hour, as well as nightly. Tourists today probably cannot reconcile the gentile Charleston they see with the wild place it was in those days when drinking, gambling, and prostitution were prevalent.

Twenty years later, the property was made into units for students at the College of Charleston. By the 1980s, it became the Battery Carriage House.

The Hauntings

I gave my first national television interview at the
Battery Carriage House. It was July, which is the
hottest month in the South Carolina Lowcountry.
Thanks to the humidity, it usually feels like 110 degrees
in the middle of the day, even in the shade. As I walked
towards the inn, sweating under the mid-day sun, my
mind was more on the unbearable heat than ghosts.

Wine, tea, and cookies are served in the lobby every afternoon.

As soon as I entered the lobby, I was approached by the producer. We exchanged brief greetings and then proceeded to Room 10, where his crew had set up their equipment. Rooms 8 and 10 are the most haunted places in the hotel. As we started the interview, it was discovered that the lighting was all wrong. When the producer asked his crew, they assured him it had been set up properly and a final check done just before my arrival. They had no explanation as to what had happened since that time. After some adjustments, we began.

Almost immediately after the interview began, we were stopped by the camera operator. He said that something was wrong and he did some fast tweaking. As soon as he finished, one of the lights that was almost directly over my head made a popping sound and went dark. The sudden and strange event was unnerving to all of us in the room. Finally, the interview was conducted. As we played back the interview, we discovered what was either audio distortion or noises in the background. We had to redo part of the interview as a result.

Afterwards, the producer assured me that this was most unusual. I think he was afraid that I would think they were unprofessional. To the contrary, I was thinking about ghosts! I was wondering if "something" didn't want us in his room. I also wondered which ghost had been the prankster.

The inn has two resident ghosts. One is known as the "Gentleman Ghost" while the other is called the "Torso Ghost."

The Gentleman Ghost is well-dressed and only shows himself to female guests. He likes to lie down beside them while they are sleeping. If a guest discovers his presence and cries out, he quickly exits through the nearest wall. It is believed to be the spirit of a college student who killed himself by jumping off the roof of this building.

The Torso Ghost is a scary sight given that he has no head! He doesn't reveal himself very often, but when he does he gives guests a real fright. He appears wearing a gray uniform and has been heard moaning, as if he is in pain. Some Confederate soldiers had to blow up an ammunitions cache before retreating so that Union soldiers couldn't get their hands on it. One of the soldiers involved died during this mission and is believed to be the Torso Ghost. He is usually seen sort of hovering over the foot of the bed in Room 8.

There have been so many reports over the years, including ones from people who did not even realize they were staying in a haunted room. Credible witnesses have reported sightings of both ghosts. One man who swore he didn't believe in ghosts (at least not before that night!) said he awoke to find "the torso of a man with no face in front of him. He said he was barrel-chested and wearing several layers of clothing." Thinking he was dreaming, he reached out and touched the garment. He recalls that it felt coarse and that he heard raspy breathing that turned into a moan when he touched the man's coat. The presence disappeared. Even though it did not harm him, he sensed it was not a benign entity.

Reports of the Gentleman Ghost are more common. He is of average build and has no distinguishable features. Sometimes he will put his arm around a female guest. Other times, he simply lies down a few inches away from the sleeping guest. This only happens in Room 10.

Some guests have tried to record their stay only to have strange things occur, such as blurred images and malfunctioning equipment—just like what happened during my interview.

While many guests never see the ghosts, they do sometimes smell cologne and hear strange noises or experience weird things in their sleeping rooms, such as lights turning on or off by themselves or the room suddenly getting very cold.

One couple had such a scary experience that they left in the middle of the night. They threw on coats over their pajamas and quickly checked out without explanation. The next morning a maid found the nightstand Bible underneath one of the bed pillows.

Visitor Information

The historic property is located in the heart of the historic district. It has ten rooms and one suite. Rooms 8 and 10 are reportedly the most haunted. Additionally, several companies offer "haunted Charleston" tours.

20 South Battery

Charleston, SC 29401

www.batterycarriagehouse.com

Charleston is five hours from Raleigh (272 miles); 13 hours from New York City (797 miles); and 5 hours from Atlanta, GA (303 miles).

St. James Hotel

St. James Hotel

FUN FACTS:

Room 18 is the most haunted room in the hotel, but no one is allowed to stay in it because the ghost has been known to push, shove, slap, and/or throw unwanted visitors into the wall.

The original owner was President Lincoln's personal chef until the president was assassinated.

The St. James was renowned for being the best hotel west of the Mississippi at one time.

The History

Henri Lambert was such a good cook that Ulysses S. Grant recommended him to become the White House chef during Abraham Lincoln's presidency. After the assassination of Lincoln, Lambert headed west to seek his fortune. Like many men of that era, the lure of a new territory and "riches beyond your wildest dreams!" was quite appealing.

He didn't strike it rich with a gold claim, but he found success as a cook. He did so well that he saved enough money to open his own place. In 1872, he opened Lambert's Saloon and Billiard Hall. As business grew, he added sleeping rooms. The renovation was well worth the investment. His property soon came to be known as one of the best hotels west of the Mississippi.

The establishment became a favorite among all sorts of men, from miners to merchants. Eventually, the Frenchman changed his name from "Henri" to "Henry" and changed the name of his place from Lambert's Saloon and Billiard Hall to The Lambert Inn, which was later renamed the St. James Hotel.

Just one look at the guest list would validate its impeccable reputation. It reads like a "who's who" of the Old West. Jessie James frequently stayed in Room 14, signing in under his alias "R.H. Howard." Buffalo Bill Cody and Annie Oakley stayed here while getting ready for their Wild West Show, a spectacular road show. According to legend, dozens of Indians accompanied them. Wyatt Earp and his family stayed several nights while en route to Tombstone, Doc Holliday, Black Jack Ketchum, Clay Allison, Bob Ford, Billy the Kid, Bat Masterson and Kit Carson. Zane Grey wrote *Fighting Caravans* and Governor Lew Wallace wrote *Ben Hur* while staying at the St. James.

With this kind of guest list, it's not surprising that the St. James saw a lot of action. There were at least two dozen men killed here during disputes that were settled the old-fashioned way—through gunfights.

The saloon is now the hotel dining room. Patrons need only look up at the ceiling to see all the bullet holes to get an idea of how many gunfights broke out here during that era.

Lambert took it all in stride. He simply added three feet of protective wood so that no one staying in the rooms located directly over the bar would get shot while sleeping!

But things always change and they changed big time once the railroad came. The need for the Santa Fe Trail disappeared once the railroad was established and the Gold Rush ended. So Cimarron lost its appeal, making it a ghost town. Henry Lambert died in 1913 and his wife, Mary, died in 1926. The St. James Hotel sat abandoned and forlorn for many years.

That changed when it was bought in 1985 and restored to its former glory. Visitors will find that little has changed at the St. James Hotel. It still has velvet window drapes, thick carpets over old wooden floors, fancy wallpaper, crystal chandeliers, an antique piano, heavy wooden chairs and tables, candelabra lamps, a pump organ, and framed photos of famous people who have stayed here over the years. As if all that doesn't transport you back to the Old West, there is a roulette table left over from the saloon era, as well as a big buffalo head mounted on the wall.

The Hauntings

The place is so inviting that some guests won't leave. The most infamous freeloader is the ghost of Thomas James "TJ" Wright. According to legend, he was playing cards one night in the second floor game room. The men had been drinking heavily and it was a high stakes game. The owner at that time was one of the participants. He felt so confident with his hand that he bet the hotel. But TJ had a better hand. Happy with his success, he called it a night. He proceeded down the hall towards his sleeping room. Just as he was about to enter Room 18, he was shot. Remarkably, he kept going across the threshold and into the room. He managed to close the door before he collapsed. Inside the locked room, Thomas James eventually bled to death.

Visitors will know right away which room this is as it has a large padlock on it because management wants to make sure that no employees or guests try to enter. Before the decision was made to close off the room once and for all, guests and staff has been shoved, pushed, knocked down, and suffered other types of violent encounters. It became obvious that TJ wanted to be left alone! While there is no official record of his death, the old registry does show that a TJ Wright stayed three nights at the St. James in 1881. We stayed at the hotel for two nights to participate in a murder mystery weekend and look for ghosts, but the owners would not allow me to enter Room 18.

Henry and Mary Lambert

The spirit of Henry Lambert's wife, Mary, is believed to linger at the St. James. Even though she died in 1926, some believe she is still here looking after guests. She is not seen but her presence has been felt often by guests, staff, and psychics. Her perfume has been smelled many times by many people. If you sleep in her old bedroom (Room 17), you may awaken to hear tapping on the window. Guests, who have left the window up to enjoy the night breeze, had heard persistent tapping until they finally close the window.

According to one investigation, two little girls who died of diphtheria and a "dwarf-sized man named "Little Imp" who steals and moves objects just to be mischievous also haunt the property.

The thing that makes St. James Hotel one of the most haunted hotels in America is that the paranormal activity is "off the charts." Guests and staff have experienced nearly all possible paranormal activity: cold spots, unexplainable electronic malfunctions, moving/falling objects, the smell of perfume and pipe smoke, footsteps, piano music is heard coming from the antique piano that hasn't been played—by humans— in years (witnesses say it sounds like old dance hall/saloon music), and the chandelier on the second floor landing turning on by itself (electricians can find no logical reason for this). The spookiest thing is the cowboy spirit. There is a mirrored bar that is original to the saloon. Patrons sometimes see the reflection of a cowboy in this mirrored surface, but when they turn around, no one is there.

While most activity occurs in the main hotel, some ghostly activity has been reported in its ten-room annex.

Visitor Information

617 South Collison Avenue

Cimarron, New Mexico 87714

www.exstjames.com

The property was sold and renovated in 2009. There are twelve rooms in the historic hotel and a two-story annex holds ten additional rooms. There is a nice restaurant and bar.

Cimarron is 93miles (90 minutes) southwest of Las Vegas, NM; 18 hours from New Orleans, LS (1,135 miles); and 8 hours from Oklahoma City, OK (500 miles).

Hotel del Coronado

Hotel Coronado

FUN FACTS:

The property celebrated its 125th anniversary in 2013.

More Presidents have visited this hotel than any other hotel in America.

This historic property is valued at approximately $600 million.

The History

One week before Christmas, three businessmen reconciled their resources to buy North Island and Coronado for $110,000. Even though that was a huge sum of money in those days, these men could afford it. Jacob Gruendike was President of First National Bank of San Diego; Hampton Story owned the Story & Clark Piano Company of Chicago; and E. Babcock was a retired railroad executive from Indiana.

They enlisted other wealthy business partners and formed the Coronado Beach Company. The company hired James W. Reid of Canada as their architect. The ground-breaking ceremony was held in March 1887.

The consortium let Reid know that they had big

plans. This was not going to be just another nice hotel. Babcock, Story, and Gruendike envisioned a grandiose resort. Reid did not disappoint them. His plans included sprawling tropical gardens, a pavilion tower, large veranda, a colonnade, and sweeping panoramic views of the Pacific Ocean. The piece-de-resistance was the Crown Room, which was constructed using only pegs and glue—not a single nail was used.

When it opened in 1888, it was the biggest resort in the world. Guests came from all over to enjoy its many luxurious amenities and activities, such as deep sea fishing and hunting expeditions.

Over the years, the Coronado has seen many changes, including an ostrich farm, Olympic-sized salt water pool, tennis courts, bowling alleys, billiards room, yacht club, and a Japanese tea garden.

Everyone from Hollywood celebrities to dignitaries have been hosted here, such as Prince Edward of Wales, Thomas Edison, Babe Ruth, Bette Davis, Rudolph Valentino, Douglas Fairbanks, Clark Gable, and Mae West. More recently, Brad Pitt, Oprah Winfrey, Whoopi Goldberg, and Barbara Streisand have stayed at the property.

The Coronado has been visited by more Presidents than any other hotel in America. Presidential visits have been made by Franklin D. Roosevelt, Woodrow Wilson, William Howard Taft, William McKinley, Dwight D. Eisenhower, John F. Kennedy, Benjamin Harrison, Lyndon B. Johnson, Richard Nixon, Gerald Ford, Jimmy Carter, Ronald Reagan, George H. Bush, George W. Bush, Bill Clinton, and Barack Obama.

Due to financial hardships, the original owners sold their shares to John D. Spreckels. During WWII, the hotel became a "wartime casualty station," and as such converted all unused acreage into vegetable gardens.

John Spreckels sold the property in 1948. It was purchased by Barney Goodman, who didn't spend much money on maintenance. By the time it was sold to John Alessio in 1960, it was in a state of disrepair. The millionaire made only necessary renovations before selling the hotel three years later. It was bought by

Larry Lawrence, who realized its potential and began making major renovations. He spent $150 million to add 700 rooms, a convention center, and two high-rises due south of the main hotel.

It was sold a couple more times and more renovations were made in 2001, 2003, and 2005, which included adding 205 guestrooms, and thirty-seven cottages and villas.

Today, the hotel is valued in the neighborhood of $600 million. But one of its biggest draws is not its guest registry or amenities or activities, but its resident ghost.

The Hauntings

According to legend, a lovely young woman checked into the hotel on November 24, 1892. She gave her name as Lottie Bernard. She was alone and had no luggage. She told staff that her brother would soon be joining her. He had stayed behind at the train station to collect their luggage.

Her brother never arrived. After three days, Bernard ventured into town where she reportedly bought a small pistol. The next morning, she was found dead on the steps that led down to the beach. She had been shot in the head, presumably a suicide.

The mystery grew as more details came out. It was discovered that her name was not Lottie Bernard but Kate Morgan. It was also discovered that she was pregnant and that she was consuming quinine. It seems that she was trying to get rid of the baby. Authorities learned that she had a husband and that the couple was scam artists who posed as brother and sister. One theory is that when her attempts to end the pregnancy had been unsuccessful, she decided to kill herself.

Regardless of the true story, strange things have occurred at the Hotel Del Coronado ever since her death that has been attributed to the ghost of Kate Morgan. Footsteps have been heard when no one is present and the curtains in the room blow even when the window is closed and there is no air circulating inside the room. Sudden temperature changes inside the room have been recorded. The television and lights turn on and off on their own. But the most obvious ghostly activity is the sightings. A young woman in a long black dress has been seen on occasion.

Some researchers tried to debunk this paranormal activity in 2007. A medium swears she spoke with this spirit who has lingered all these years waiting for someone to discover the truth about her identity, which is Charlotte Barnard from Detroit. But none of this can be positively verified, so the mystery lingers...as well as the ghost sightings at the Hotel del Coronado.

Visitor Information

The property encompasses twenty-eight oceanfront acres that are located on a peninsula across the bay from San Diego. The gorgeous Victorian seaside resort became a National Historic Landmark in 1977. Guests can dine in its award-winning restaurant or stay in one of its deluxe rooms, villas, or cottages.

1500 Orange Avenue

Coronado, CA 92118

www.hoteldel.com

Coronado is 2.5 hours from Los Angeles (135 miles); 11 hours from Salt Lake City, UT (750 miles) and 8 hours from San Francisco (500 miles).

Grove Park Inn

Grove Park Inn

FUN FACTS:

The Pink Lady haunts this hotel, especially Room 545.

This resort hotel was largely constructed using stones that weigh as much as 10,000 pounds.

Grove set a deadline for the hotel to be ready in less than one year. Men lived in tents on the grounds and worked more than twelve hours a day, six days a week to achieve his goal.

Edwin W. Grove

The History

The historic Grove Park Inn was built by a man who got rich selling Chill Tonic. Edwin Grove was the owner of Grove's Pharmacy & Paris Medicine Company. He made millions off this elixir, but it didn't cure his respiratory condition. His doctor suggested he spend summers in the North Carolina mountains. The pure, mountain air and climate would be good for his chronic bronchitis, the physician told him.

Not only did Asheville restore his health, Grove loved the area. He returned summer after summer until he got the idea to build a hotel here. It was designed to look like the grand hotels that had been built along the railroad.

The problem was that this hotel was being built on top of a mountain. Mules, ropes, pulleys, and wagons had to be used to transport the heavy stones up on the mountain. Some weighed as much as 10,000 pounds.

Grove wanted the hotel completed in less than a year. In order to achieve this lofty goal, 400 men were hired. They were paid high wages in exchange for working long hours, which was upwards of twelve hours a day, six days a week.

Nevertheless, the men got the job done. The hotel was done just three days short of the one year deadline. The Grove Park Inn officially opened for business on July 12, 1913.

The hotel has ten floors and more than 500 guest rooms and suites. In addition to the usual amenities: lounges, tennis courts, golf course, dining room, meeting space, and two ballrooms, the property has some unusual amenities. One of its most unique features is an elevator that was incorporated into one of the enormous lobby fireplace chimneys. Guests feel like they are disappearing into the mountain as the doors close and they are whisked upstairs.

Another outstanding feature is the hotel's 40,000-square foot subterranean spa. In addition to fireplaces, a waterfall pool, café, and a mineral pool, patrons can choose from close to five dozen treatment options. *Travel and Leisure* selected it as one of the World's Best Spas.

Like many grand old hotels, the Grove Park Inn has accommodated lots of famous guests, such as Magician/Illusionist Harry Houdini, President Richard Nixon, Inventor Thomas Edison, Tycoon John D. Rockefeller, Comedian Jerry Seinfeld, and Author F. Scott Fitzgerald. In fact, Fitzgerald lived in the hotel for two years while his wife was seeking treatment in a nearby insane asylum.

The Hauntings

One guest that has never checked-out is the Pink Lady. Although she has been seen and heard from many times over the years, not much is known about her. What we do know is that a young woman wearing a fancy pink ball gown plummeted to her death during the 1920s. She had been staying in Room 545 when she fell over the hall balcony into the Palm Court Atrium. Theories have emerged that include accidental death, suicide, and murder.

Some believe she was seeing a married man. When she got pregnant, he wasn't happy. He may have pushed her over the railing to terminate his problem. But that is only speculation, as far as I know that is no evidence as to who she was or whether she jumped or was pushed from the fifth floor.

What is indisputable is all the paranormal activity that has been reported over the years. Some claim to have seen a lady in pink while others report that it is more of a thick, pinkish smoke that resembles a wispy figure rather than an unmistakable female being. Most have felt an unseen presence rather than see it, such as something sitting on the bed or behind them in the hallway.

The elevator is often summoned to the fifth floor but no one is on there when the doors open. Lights turn on and off, closet doors are opened and closed, and blankets have been pulled off guests during the night. Bathrooms and sleeping rooms have been found locked from the inside, which is impossible given that the door must be locked from the inside. Employees and guests have reported cold spots and strange sensations while in certain areas of the hotel.

Ghostly investigations have revealed unmistakable paranormal activity, especially in Room 545 and the main part of the inn.

Visitor Information

290 Macon Avenue

Asheville, NC 28807

https://www.omnihotels.com/hotels/asheville-grove-park

Asheville is 9.5 hours from Jackson, Mississippi (575 miles); 4 hours from Charleston, SC (262 miles); and 9 hours from Memphis, TN (500 miles).

Lemp Mansion Restaurant & Inn

Lemp Mansion Restaurant & Inn

FUN FACTS:

Some believe the house is cursed, which explains why four family members committed suicide.

By the 1860s there were 40 breweries in the St. Louis area taking advantage of the caves along the Mississippi with the Lemp family's Western Brewery being the most successful.

The place is reportedly haunted by the Lemp family.

The History

The Lemp Mansion dates back to the early 1860's. It was bought by William J. Lemp, who used it as both a residence and office. Lemp owned a prosperous brewery down the street and used part of his home as auxiliary office space.

There was certainly plenty of space given that the Victorian mansion had thirty-three rooms. Modern day conveniences made the place all the more desirable. A radiator system was installed in the late 1880s, just a few years after radiant heat was invented. A large open-style elevator was installed for easy access to the entire house.

Despite these changes, the house maintained an "old world" charm. This is largely due to the Italian marble mantles, hand-painted ceilings, and woodwork carved out of mahogany. An impressive art collection was displayed throughout the house.

The house boasts some unusual features, as well. There is an observation deck and skylights on the third floor, an auditorium and theater (actors were often hired to perform vaudeville skits), and a swimming pool was built inside the underground cavern. It has long been sealed off, but at one time there was a tunnel that extended from the basement to the brewery. Hot water was obtained from the brewery's boiler house to heat the underground pool.

The brewery was founded by William J. Lemp's father, John Adam Lemp. He was a German immigrant who established a plant that produced vinegar and beer and operated a small pub that beside the plant. He created the first lager beer in St. Louis and it was considered to be a premium beer. It sold so well that he abandoned vinegar production, focusing solely on the Lemp Western Brewing Co.

William Lemp Sr. built a new plant in 1864 that extended the length of five city blocks. By 1870, this was the largest brewery in St. Louis and the Lemps were one of the wealthiest families in the area. In 1892, the brewery was renamed the William J. Lemp Brewing Company. Five years later, William's daughter, Hilda, married Gustav Pabst of Pabst Brewing Company of Milwaukee. What a fortuitous union!

Despite their success in business, the family suffered from many personal problems. William's son, Frederick, died mysteriously at the age of 28 (some accounts list his age at time of death as 42). His death was a result of heart failure, but it is unclear why this occurred at such a young age and no family history of heart problems.

Other problems drove William into semi-seclusion. He still went into work daily, but he used the tunnel system to get to the brewery and back to the house. Records indicate that while he continued to go to work, he did not have much interest in the brewery anymore. On February 13, 1904, he got up, got dressed, ate breakfast, and then went upstairs and killed himself.

William J. Lemp Jr. took over the brewery. Unfortunately, he was not as good at making money as he was at spending it. He and his wife, Lillian, built multiple homes and spent large sums of money on fancy carriages, artwork, servants, and clothes. Eventually, they grew tired of one another and ended their marriage with a scandalous divorce.

That was just the beginning of William's troubles. His mother died at home in 1906 from cancer. That same year, nine competing breweries formed an alliance called the Independent Breweries Company. This drastically hurt the Lemp brewery, as did World War I.

When Prohibition took hold in 1919 that was the final straw for the brewery, which was already in disrepair due to lack of money to properly maintain and update machinery. William saw the writing on the wall and sold the business for pennies on the dollar. He sold the legendary "Falstaff" logo to another brewery for a mere $25,000 and sold the entire brewery for $588,000.

It had been valued at $7 million in the years preceding Prohibition.

Troubles kept coming for the family. Elsa Lemp Wright committed suicide in 1920, although some are not sure it was suicide. This further fueled William's depression. On December 29, 1922, he shot himself with a .38 caliber revolver. The funeral was held at the Lemp Mansion.

He was survived by two brothers, Charles and Edwin. Charles moved into the Lemp Mansion. He lived alone in the big, old house except for two servants. He killed himself on May 10, 1949. He was the only Lemp family member to leave a suicide note, but all it said was not to blame anyone for his death. Reportedly, he killed his beloved dog before shooting himself.

Edwin Lemp was one of the few family members to die of old age. He died in 1970 at age 90 of natural causes. His final instructions included that all of the Lemp family artwork, artifacts, and documents be destroyed. Everything was burned in an enormous bonfire. I wonder if he thought this might end the family "curse?"

After Edwin died, the property was sold and converted into a boarding house, which was allowed to deteriorate. This may explain why it was hard to find tenants. Or maybe there is another explanation…

The Hauntings

Once Lemp Mansion became a boarding house, tenants began complaining about strange noises, including unexplainable footsteps and knocking. It was hard to keep tenants for any period of time.

The property was purchased in 1975 by Dick Pointer. The family began renovating the house. During the time, contractors complained of tools being moved, unexplainable noises, and the feeling of being watched by an unseen presence.

This continues today. Staff and patrons of the

inn's restaurant have seen glasses fly through the air and hear unexplainable noises. Guests of the inn have reported their fair share of paranormal activity. Some swear they have seen a female apparition that is believed to be Lillian Lemp, the "Lavender Lady." They have heard the piano but no one is playing it, heard muffled voices, and have had doors lock and unlock on their own.

Guests have seen a ghost dog and had what feels like a dog rubbing up against their leg while in the hallway of the third floor. It is believed to be Charles Lemp's dog. Other haunted areas are the bedroom where William Jr. killed himself, the room where Charles killed himself (now the bar), and the third floor bedroom where William Sr. killed himself.

Note: While Elsa Lemp did commit suicide, it did not happen in this house.

Since the Lemp mansion was the location of so much tragedy, it is no wonder that so much paranormal activity occurs here.

It has been investigated by many ghost groups, including Ghost Lab, Fear, Ghost Hunters, Off Limits, and TAPS with paranormal activity indicated in every investigation.

Visitor Information

3322 DeMenil Place

St. Louis, Missouri 63118

www.lempmansion.com

The Lemp Mansion is an inn and restaurant. It also offers history/ghost tours, as well as dinner theatre and special seasonal events. There is a gift shop and museum on site, which features many personal items once owned by the Lemp family and Lemp Brewery memorabilia.

St. Louis is 5.5 hours from Chicago, IL (300 miles); 6.5 hours from Columbus, OH (400 miles); and 10 hours from Pittsburgh, PA (606 miles).

Marshall House Hotel

Marshall House Hotel

FUN FACTS:

The staff keeps a notebook of all reported paranormal activity.

During renovations, body parts were found hidden under the floorboards.

Joel Chandler Harris lived here while writing Uncle Remus. The sound of typing is heard sometimes coming from the room where he stayed.

The History

The Marshall House Hotel is the oldest hotel in Savannah, dating back to 1851. It was built by Gabriel Leaver, who bought a lot of land and properties throughout Savannah after realizing its economic potential. When he died, his daughter, Mary Marshall, inherited all these properties.

The hotel's signature iron veranda was added in 1857. A major renovation was done two years later. Business was booming until the Civil War when the hotel was commandeered by General William Sherman. He converted it into a Union hospital.

By the turn of the century, the hotel had running hot water on every floor and electric lights. It had also changed ownership several times and sat vacant for a few years. The place also saw major renovations in 1941, 1998, and 2008.

It has been a National Historic Building since 2000. The hotel still boasts its original wood floors, fireplaces, and staircases. The iron veranda you see today is an exact replica of the original.

The Hauntings

Guests have reported being awakened during the night by rattling doorknobs, but no one is there when they open the door to see who is trying to get into their room. Loud crashes have been heard coming from the fourth floor in the early morning hours, but nothing and no one is ever found when someone investigates.

Guests have heard water running in the bathroom. When they go into the bathroom to check it out, they find the faucet has been turned on in the bathtub.

Some guests swear their wrists have been grabbed or touched during the night, but no one is there when they open their eyes. Many wonder if this isn't the spirit of one of the nurses who is still checking for a patient's pulse.

The spirits of male soldiers have been seen by employees and workman in the basement. The apparitions are carrying stretchers with mutilated bodies on them. A ghostly figure has been seen near the main floor restrooms, hallways, and entry on many occasions. A one-armed Union soldier has been seen walking through the lobby carrying his amputated arm.

These sightings and strange happenings make sense given its history as a Civil War hospital. During the winter of 1864, it was too cold and the ground was too hard to dig graves, so resourceful doctors "buried" body parts under the floorboards.

Many soldiers suffered injuries that resulted in amputations. The surgeries usually took place in the basement and were often nothing more than sawing off arms and legs. The remains of these body parts have been discovered during renovations.

It was also used as a hospital during two yellow fever epidemics that wiped out much of Savannah's population, including many children. This could explain the sounds of children running and playing in the hallways when no children are even staying at the hotel.

Today, the Marshall House Hotel is a beautiful and convenient place to stay in the heart of Savannah's Historic District. During the mid-1800's, however, it was the site of much pain and suffering and sadness. Many believe the ghosts of the soldiers who were brought here during the Civil War linger here, as well as the spirits of nurses who are still making rounds.

Visitor Information

123 E. Broughton Street

Savannah, GA 31401

www.marshallhouse.com

Savannah is 2.5 hours from Columbia, SC (158 miles); 4 hours from Atlanta, GA (248 miles); and 5 hours from Raleigh, NC (321 miles).

The hotel does permit people to explore the premises— even if they are not guests. There is a nice on-site restaurant and a haunted hotel package is offered, as well as other options.

Terrance Zepke

Farnsworth House Inn

Farnsworth House Inn

FUN FACTS:

This house played an important role during the Battle of Gettysburg.

There is a séance room and Mourning Theater.

Five of its nine guest rooms are haunted.

The History

The original house was made of wood and completed in 1810. Twenty-three years later, a three-story brick addition was added onto the dwelling. This made the already substantial house an impregnable structure.

Soldiers thought so too. During the Civil War, Confederate soldiers sent sharp shooters up to the attic of this house to pluck off Union soldiers up on Cemetery Hill. The hill was only 100 yards or so from the house and crawling with soldiers during the infamous Battle of Gettysburg. Seeing the potential danger, the family fled the house.

However, there was a civilian casualty when a bullet came through a wall of a neighbor's house and hit a young woman while she was baking bread in her kitchen.

The Battle of Gettysburg was a turning point in the Civil War. It was fought July 1 – 3, 1863 in and around the town of Gettysburg. This battle involved the largest number of casualties of the entire Civil War. The most intense fighting, Pickett's Charge, occurred on the third day when nearly 13,000 Confederate soldiers attacked the Union on Cemetery Hill. General Robert E. Lee suffered great losses during this battle and it was the beginning of the end for the Confederates.

It was during this assault that Union forces exchanged heavy fire with the Confederate snipers stationed inside this house. They had to get rid of the sharpshooters if they had any hope of winning this battle. They achieved their goal and all the Confederate snipers were dead by the end of the day, as well as the civilian who died from the stray bullet.

After this battle, Union troops, who had realized the usefulness of the sturdy structure and its key location, commandeered it as their headquarters. By the time the Sweeny family was allowed to return to their residence, more than 100 bullet holes marred the south wall of the brick side of the house.

In the early 1900s, the house was converted into an inn, the Farnsworth House Inn. It was named in honor of Union General John Farnsworth who died in battle.

The Farnsworth House Inn is on the National Register of Historic Places. Guests can choose from nine different guest rooms with at least five being known to be haunted. Victorian era antiques and Civil War memorabilia can be found throughout the inn.

The Hauntings

It has been investigated by many people over the years, as have many other places in Gettysburg. The most haunted places in the former house are the attic, basement, and three guest rooms: Eisenhower Room, Longstreet Room, and Sara Black Room. The first two can be reserved by guests but the Sara Black Room is unavailable for any paranormal investigations. However, you can see a photograph that was taken in 1999 that shows an apparition floating above the bed in the Sara Black Room.

The inn is haunted by as many as fourteen ghosts. One is an elderly woman who is usually seen in the hallway between the tavern and kitchen. She is believed to be a former owner or cook or kitchen help.

Another is 'Mary' who was a midwife and appears to guests who she believes needs comforting. A video filmed in 2008 captured paranormal activity including a female spirit with red-hair piled up on her head in an old-fashioned hair style standing in the doorway of the room. Could this be Mary or another spirit?

'Jeremy' is a mischievous boy who was run over

by a horse and buggy while playing in front of the inn. Previous guests have brought toys and set them out for Jeremy at bedtime and have found them in a different location in the morning.

A man wearing clothing from the late 1800s has been seen in the hallways, but his identity is unknown. Civil War soldier spirits have been seen too. In addition to sightings, guests have experienced a wide range of paranormal activity, such as:

*coming back to their room to find their beds messed up and pillows strewn about

*wooden chair in room creaks and moves as if someone is in it rocking back and forth

*doors opening and closing

*smell of tobacco smoke

*room suddenly gets very cold

*hair is pulled or tugged

*guest is pinched

*unseen presence stroking hand during the night

*hear music coming from the attic

*moving shadows

*footsteps

*thumping coming from the attic late at night

Visitor Information

401 Baltimore Street

Gettysburg, Pennsylvania 17325

www.farnsworthhouseinn.com

There are several options for visitors, including a Civil War Mourning Theater Show. It is offered nightly in the spooky cellar of the Farnsworth Inn. Ghost stories are shared by a costumed storyteller, as well as interesting tales pertaining to the Battle of Gettysburg and there is live music too. I highly recommend it. Other options include paranormal nights, ghost walks, séance room, and history tours of the house (weekends only). Next door is a walk-through haunted attraction that is open daily. It is a "house of horrors with special effects that depicts scenes of actual Gettysburg haunting events."

If you're planning an overnight stay, keep in mind that Gettysburg is a very popular tourist attraction and so all lodging tends to book up, especially during summer and special events, such as re-enactments. Reserve your room well in advance of your stay and remember that half the rooms available for overnight guests are reportedly haunted, so your chance of a ghostly encounter are good!

Gettysburg is 8 hours from Asheville, NC (495 miles); 6.5 hours from Columbus, OH (350 miles); and 15 hours from Memphis, TN (900 miles).

Terrance Zepke

Crescent Hotel

Crescent Hotel

FUN FACTS:

This place has been dubbed the "Grand Old Lady of the Ozarks."

This place was built in large part by expert stone masons imported from Ireland.

The hotel has been many things over the years, including a hospital, summer resort, and college for women.

The History

Located in the heart of the Ozark Mountains, the Crescent Hotel was designed by a renowned architect, Isaac Taylor. Construction began in 1884 on 27 acres at the north rim of West Mountain. The owners, who included a former governor of Arkansas and railroad executives, deliberately chose the location because of nearby Eureka Springs.

The springs were believed to contain healing minerals, which brought people from all over America seeking help for various afflictions. A bottling facility was established so that the pure spring water could be bottled, shipped, and sold across America.

Since the hotel was catering to the affluent, no detail was considered too insignificant. Premium limestone was used for the exterior. Stone masons were imported from Ireland. These expert masons built walls that were close to two feet thick, multiple towers, elaborate balconies, and an enormous fireplace in the lobby.

It took two years to complete "The Grand Old Lady of the Ozarks," as the resort has become affectionately known. It had every creature comfort from the modern plumbing and steam heat to extensive landscaping and impeccable furnishings. The cost totaled nearly $300,000, which was an exorbitant amount back in the 1800s.

When it opened on May 5, 1886 some publications called it the best resort in America. Sadly, by the early 1900s, folks had realized that Eureka Springs had no curative powers and stopped coming to the resort.

The hotel was converted into the Crescent College and Conservatory for Young Women in 1908. The tuition was very costly due to the prestige of the school and the cost to maintain the property. For that reason, the school was only in operation a few years. For the next few years, it became a junior college.

When the age of the automobile arrived, it made the old hotel accessible to far more people. Reportedly, more than 500,000 guests stayed here during 1929, including some businesses who leased it as a summer resort.

The place was sold to Norman Baker in 1937. He had a plan to turn the hotel into a hospital and health clinic. Baker claimed to have learned how to cure cancer. He and another scam artist, Harry Hoxsey, opened the Baker Institute in Muscatine, Iowa. Reportedly, the facility was raking in as much as $100,000 a month. The AMA opened criticized his expensive treatments as being worthless. In 1930, he and Hoxsey had been charged with practicing medicine without a license. Baker ended up paying a small fine and serving only one day in jail. A few years later, he bought the Crescent Hotel and opened his cancer-curing resort hospital.

Baker nearly destroyed the character of the Grand Old Lady of the Ozarks when he tore down balconies and repainted using gaudy shades of orange, red, and black. He moved into the penthouse, which he painted psychedelic purple.

Crescent Hotel, Eureka Springs, Ark.

He made a fortune off the clinic. One of Baker's "cures" for a brain tumor was to cut the patient's scalp and pour a mixture of Eureka Springs water and ground watermelon seeds into the opening. He swindled sick folks out of a total of four million dollars. Worse than the financial loss was the suffering and death that resulted from his worthless remedies. The law caught up with the shady businessman and he was charged with fraud. He was found guilty and sentenced to four years in prison. The hotel "clinic" shut down.

New investors were found and much needed renovations were done. The hotel reopened in 1946. In 1997, the property was bought by Marty and Elise Roenigk. They added a 6,500-square foot spa they named "New Moon Spa", which includes Vichy showers, hydrotherapy, a sauna, and more. Extensive renovations have been done to the property, including the penthouse, observation tower, and signature twenty-four-foot weathervane. There are fifteen acres of formal gardens and nature trails. Guests can choose to stay in one of the seventy-two guest rooms or twelve suites.

The Hauntings

There are many haunted areas and rooms throughout the inn, including the dining room, lobby, bar area, hallways, basement, and Rooms 424, 218, 202, and 419. One of the ghosts is believed to be the spirit of an Irish stone mason who died when he fell off the roof while helping to build the hotel. He fell near where Room 218 is located. Guests have complained of hearing footsteps outside their door, pounding on the wall, and being shaken by an unseen presence during the night.

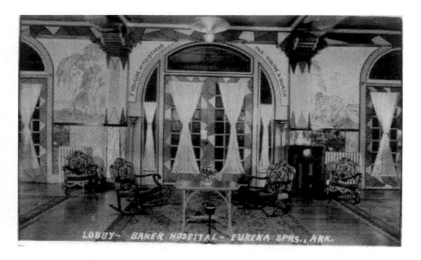

A nice-looking man with a beard and mustache has been seen wearing Victorian era clothing. He only appears in the lobby or bar. He sits quietly as if lost in thought or perhaps waiting for someone and then at some point he simply vanishes.

A spirit known as Theodosia is seen in Room 419. She is believed to be a cancer patient who died while under Dr. Baker's care. She appears most often to housekeepers when they are in Room 419. The eeriest sight is probably the one that is usually seen after 11 p.m. Guests and employees have seen a nurse pushing a gurney down the hallway. They watch in amazement as the nurse and gurney disappear into the wall at the end of the hall. Dozens of people have claimed to have witnessed this sight over the years.

Research reveals that the bodies of deceased cancer patients were discreetly moved after 11 p.m. Even those who say they didn't see anything report hearing the sounds of squeaking and creaking outside their rooms, as if someone was pushing a cart down the hall. However, no one is in the hall when the guest investigates the noise.

Near the foot of the stairs to the old recreation room, a figure has been seen that is believed to be "Dr." Baker. The shadowy figure looks like it is wearing a white coat, similar to a doctor's jacket. The front desk used a switchboard system at one time, but it hasn't been active in years. The owners wanted to keep the antique switchboard for posterity but were forced to remove it. They said they had to because the front desk kept getting calls on the switchboard, which was stored in the old recreation room in the basement. However, that room was kept locked and was not used anymore. Whenever they went to find out what was going on, the employees could not find anyone or anything to explain the calls. The door was always locked and there is no other way in or out of that room. The only key was kept at the front desk. Sometimes a second call was received at the front desk within minutes of investigating the initial call! Finally, these unexplained incidents upset the staff so much that they refused to go down to the basement anymore.

DINING ROOM, BAKER HOSPITAL, EUREKA SPRS., ARK.

The Dining Room is one of the most haunted places in the hotel. Objects, such as chairs, silverware, and menus, are often moved. During the holidays, a giant Christmas tree is brought into the dining room and presents are placed underneath it. Often times, the gifts are found in a neat pile on the other side of the room from the tree.

The place is believed to be haunted by the spirits of the people who died here. During renovations, human skeletal remains were found. According to legend, Baker hid the bodies of the patients who died while under his care all over the property. Since he was claiming to cure cancer, he couldn't let others know that people were dying instead of recovering. Critically-ill patients were put into an asylum ward so that their deaths would not be discovered by other patients.

Visitor Information

75 Prospect Place

Eureka Springs, Arkansas 72632

www.crescent-hotel.com

Eureka Springs is in the far northwest corner of Arkansas, just eight miles south of the Missouri border near Beaver Lake.

Eureka Springs is 5.5 hours from Memphis, TN (323 miles); 3.5 hours from Little Rock, AK (188 miles); and 7 hours from Lincoln, NE (424 miles).

Bullock Hotel

Bullock Hotel

FUN FACTS:

Visitors can drink, eat, shop, gamble, and chase ghosts while at the Bullock Hotel. As of November 1, 1989, Deadwood is only place in the U.S. outside of Nevada and Atlantic City where gambling is completely legal.

It is haunted by its original owner, Seth Bullock.

This was the first hotel in Deadwood. In 1887, the first slot machines were invented and soon thereafter installed at the Bullock.

The History

Deadwood was established during the Black Hills Gold Rush. Gold was first discovered in a narrow canyon in the Black hills that became known as Deadwood Gulch. Men came from near and far in search of their fortunes. This resulted in a surge of saloons and dance halls, gambling halls, and brothels. As the time grew, it morphed from shacks and tents to wood, stone, and brick buildings.

Sheriff Seth Bullock kept the peace, which was no easy task in a frontier town full of prostitutes, miners, merchants, and cowboys. The challenges grew as the railroad arrived at Deadwood in 1890. The city has grown and changed a great deal over the years, but has managed to maintain its small town charm. Deadwood was named a National Historic Landmark in 1964. It was the first community to be designated as such. The last house of ill repute, Pam's Purple Door, closed in 1980.

Seth Bullock had arrived in Deadwood one day after Wild Bill Hickok was shot and killed while playing cards. This made folks realize how out of control things were in Deadwood, so they asked Bullock to take authority since he was a retired lawman. He became the first sheriff of this town.

In the late 1890s, Seth Bullock built a hardware store and warehouse. He was a good businessman and he prospered until a fire quickly burned down the wooden building. He chose to build a hotel on the site of the former hardware store.

The design is an eclectic and unusual blend of Italianate and Victorian architectural styles. The main level held a large dining room, kitchen, pantry, offices, and a grand lobby. Sixty-three guest rooms encompassed the second and third floors. The Branch House was added at a later date. It is adjacent to the hotel and offers seven deluxe suites.

Ironically, when the hotel was sold in 1976, the new owner converted the store into a hotel. In 1991, it was sold again and the new owner converted it back into a hotel.

Renovations have been made but the integrity of the
original hotel has been preserved as much as possible.
However, the kitchen and pantry were made into a
restaurant and bar. Also, the renovations decreased the
number of rooms from 63 to 28. The original rooms
were just too tiny by today's standards.

The Hauntings

The original owner, Seth Bullock, died in the hotel on September 23, 1919 in Room 211. Some reports contradict this claim saying that he died at his home. Regardless which story is true, it is believed that he haunts the property. Several paranormal groups who have conducted official investigations concur. The former owner usually only makes his presence known when staff is goofing off or not doing their job properly. He will remind them to get to work by touching them on the shoulder or arm or by tugging on their clothing, but employees say they are aware of his presence long before he interacts with them. They swear they can sense his presence and know it's time to get back to work.

If his unseen presence is not enough to motivate employees, he has been known to move cleaning carts and bar stools, as well as throw plates and glasses in the kitchen. If that is not enough to do the trick, a disembodied male voice has been heard calling out an employee's name. Sometimes, a man's footsteps approaching and whistling are also heard.

Seth Bullock

Sometimes, the letter "A" is seen in the mirror on the second floor. Guests have captured it on film but no one has any idea what it is about. One theory is that Seth Bullock was notorious for telling his staff to be "Absolute" (as in give the task your absolute best effort) and that he is still trying to send that message.

The most common paranormal activity is heavy footsteps that seem to be stomping and objects put on the dresser are sometimes found elsewhere in the guest room.

The ghost of a girl called Sarah loves shiny objects, so if you leave coins or jewelry in your room, you may find it has been moved. But don't worry, she has never stolen anything!

Visitor Information

633 Main Street

Deadwood, South Dakota 57732

www.historicbullock.com

In addition to lodging, the property features a nice restaurant and casino. They offer ghost tours and special events seasonally.

Deadwood is 6 hours from Denver, CO (373 miles); 11 hours from Dodge City, KS (666 miles); and 20 hours from San Antonio, TX (1,277 miles).

Adolphus Hotel

Adolphus Hotel

FUN FACTS:

When the hotel was built in the early 1900s, it was superior to all other commercial buildings in Dallas.

It is haunted by a ghost bride.

Many additions have been made to the property over the years in an effort to accommodate an ever-increasing demand.

The History

The world renowned hotel was the brainchild of Adolphus Busch. He envisioned a luxury hotel and had the capital to achieve his goal since he owned Busch Beer Company. Construction began in 1910 and the property opened for business two years later.

The hotel was everything Busch dreamed of. Not only because it turned out so well, but because it was more sophisticated than other commercial properties that existed in downtown Dallas at that time. The granite, brick, and stone building featured a baroque design and was topped with a multi-colored French mansard roof, which included a large turret. Roman statutes stood imposingly on the ledges all around the fifteenth-story.

The inside was equally impressive with dark wood-paneled walls that came from Caucus Mountains walnut trees. The paneling was inlaid with gold. Lush carpeting, a massive lobby staircase, and a high domed ceiling in the Palm Garden and oversized windows offered panoramic views of downtown Dallas. Antique frescoes and tapestries hung on the walls and a beautiful Steinway lend a wonderful 'Old World' atmosphere.

Word got around fast about this boutique hotel and soon they were turning down business. They needed to expand to keep up with demand, so by 1916, renovations underway to add an annex on the west side of the property. The addition included a fabulous rooftop restaurant. The eatery was dubbed "Bambooland" because it consisted of bamboo walls and fancy Oriental furnishings. Within a few years, another addition was done to accommodate the ever growing demand. When it was completed, the hotel had 825 guest rooms.

The Adolphus has hosted many distinguished guests over the years, ranging from dignitaries to celebrities. The list of who's who includes names such as Queen Elizabeth and Prince Phillip, President Roosevelt, President Carter, President Reagan, and President George H.W. Bush. In addition to the famous people it has hosted, many legendary performers have played here, such as Tommy Dorsey, Glenn Miller, and Benny Goodman.

Adolphus Busch

The Hauntings

Guests will enjoy all kinds of amenities and may even encounter a ghost or two! Patrons have complained about footsteps and muffled conversations taking place outside their rooms all hours of the night. But no one is there when they open the door to confront the noisy guests. There have also been complaints about being disturbed late at night by Big Band music, but management always assures the irate guest that there is no band rehearsing or performing anywhere in the hotel at that time. Some guests swear they hear a woman sobbing and ask staff to find her and help her. However, employees never find a woman in such a state.

These reports usually come from guests staying on the nineteenth floor, which used to be the Palm Garden. The ballroom, however, was sealed off during renovations that took place in 1979. The sobbing woman who is often heard is believed to be a former patron. A woman used to frequent the hotel's bistro. After her death, employees swore they often saw her sitting at her favorite table. When they cross the room to get a closer look, the woman vanishes.

Overnight employees claim to hear doors slamming and see doors opening on their own. Some have witnessed windows flying open. Housekeepers have been tapped on their shoulders while cleaning, especially when they are cleaning the lobby restrooms. Bartenders swear that a playful spirit likes to move beer bottles. When the bartender restocks beer, he lines up the bottles in a row. The last bottle in the row is often moved out of place. When the bartender moves it back into the row, he soon finds it moved out of place again. This goes on for a while before the bartender gives up and leaves it where the ghost wants it to be.

Over the years, many have been adamant about feeling an unseen presence. They aren't the only ones. According to long-time employee and restaurant manager, Louis Ford, patrons often mention feeling like someone is watching them.

But the most famous ghost at the Adolphus is the ghost bride. During the 1930s, a young man was abandoned at the altar. She waited and waited but her fiancé never showed up for the ceremony. Later, she learned that he had gotten cold feet and couldn't face her. Some reports indicate that she hanged herself in what would have been their honeymoon suite. Others say that she leaped off the hotel to her death. Regardless of how she died, her death is well documented—and so are the hauntings. She has been seen dozens of times over the years wandering the halls in a shimmery white dress that looks like a wedding gown.

Visitor Information

1321 Commerce Street

Dallas, Texas 75202

www.adolphus.com

Dallas is 5 hours from Little Rock, Arkansas (320 miles); 19 hours from Raleigh, NC (1,200 miles); and 10 hours from Albuquerque, New Mexico (650 miles).

Hotel San Carlos

Hotel San Carlos

When it was built, the hotel was the tallest building in the city. It also was the first to have an elevator and air conditioning.

The hotel is featured in the opening scene of Alfred Hitchcock's creepiest cult classic, Psycho (1960).

There are three resident ghosts.

The History

The first school built in Phoenix, Arizona was a four-room adobe building. It was erected in 1874 on the site of an old Native American Indian settlement. Five years later, a bigger school replaced the modest structure. Several additions were made to the school before it was condemned in 1916.

The land was sold to the Babbitt family (as in former Secretary of Interior and Governor of Arizona, Bruce Babbitt). They sold the land to Dwight Heard and Charles Harris, who built the San Carlos Hotel.

The hotel was designed by celebrated architect, George W. Ritchie. The Italian Renaissance style hotel was the first in the city to have air conditioning, which was most welcome in the hot and humid Southwest desert. This contributed significantly to the hefty $850,000 construction costs.

Other noteworthy features include Austrian crystal chandeliers and wall sconces, copper-clad doors and moldings, terra cotta tiles in the entrance, and carved crown molding in the lobby. At one time, it was the tallest building in the city and had the first elevator. The original steam heat radiator system is still being used.

The San Carlos Hotel opened its doors on March 19, 1928. To recoup their investment, the owners charged a $1 more per day than the normal hotel room rate. Appreciative patrons thought the A/C was well worth the higher rate.

Many Hollywood stars frequented the property.

Clark Gable always stayed in Room 412. During his love affair with Carole Lombard she often stayed here too. So did Marilyn Monroe, Gene Autry, Jack Dempsey, John F. Kennedy, Cary Grant, Humphrey Bogart, Jean Harlow, and Spencer Tracy. These are just a few of the many movie stars and politicians who stayed in the hotel from 1928 – 1966. The two-room suites have been named in honor of these famous guests, such as the Marilyn Monroe suite.

During World War II, troops were housed here. The bar was nicknamed "Base Operations" because more officers could be found in this bar than at Luke Air Force Base.

There's an interesting story about the hotel's penthouse. Charles Harris was half owner of the hotel at one time. He lived in the penthouse along with his wife, Elsie, and their two sons. When he died, the family moved out of the hotel penthouse. New management had planned to rent the penthouse to special guests, such as politicians and celebrities. However, that never happened. For unknown reasons, the penthouse was never made available to anyone. No one has lived in it since the Harris family, but renovations are always being done to the penthouse.

The hotel was added to the National Register of Historic Places in 1983. The 128-room property also has the honor of being the only boutique hotel in continuous use since it opened in 1928. More than $1 million in renovations were done in 2003, but the hotel still boasts most of its original antique fixtures and furnishings.

The Hauntings

The San Carlos Hotel has at least three ghosts. One is the ghost of Leone Johnson. She is probably the most famous spirit of San Carlos. She was also the first recorded suicide. Just two months after the hotel opened, the twenty-two-year-old jumped off the roof to end her life. She had been wearing a lovely white ball gown. Some speculate that she was jilted by a lover and the grief drove her to commit suicide. Whatever the reason, guests have reported sightings of a "white cloud" ever since that night. Whenever a sighting occurs, a "breeze" accompanies it.

Some claim to have witnessed the ghost of a little girl, but there is no record as to who she is or how she died. Her giggle and small footsteps have been heard and her presence felt by guests.

According to legend, three or four little boys died during the late1890's. The hotel's water supply came from a well. The boys drowned in this well while playing. After this incident, the old school was condemned as being "unsafe" and put up for sale. The sounds of boys laughing and running can be heard when no children are around.

The well, located in the basement of the hotel, is still used today. In fact, guests often question the staff about the water because it tastes so good and pure. The San Carlos Hotel is the only building in Phoenix that is not connected to the city's water supply.

Another person committed suicide by jumping off the roof in 2004, but doesn't appear to haunt the place. Some speculate that at least one spirit may result from the hotel being built on a former Hohokam Indian settlement, but there is no evidence of that either.

Years of strange events have led the staff to work on the buddy system. Housekeepers and maintenance men work in teams of two or three.

Visitor Information

202 North Central Avenue

Phoenix, Arizona 85004

www.hotelsancarlos.com

The hotel is located in downtown Phoenix, which is 5.5 hours from San Diego, CA (395 miles); 11 hours from Salt Lake City, UT (686 miles); and 12 hours from Reno, NV (737 miles).

Fun Quiz

1. Which actor/comedian haunts the Chateau Marmont?
2. Name the best-selling book (that was made into a Hollywood movie) that was inspired by paranormal activity witnessed by the author.
3. Which one of the places discussed in this book is haunted by a ghost dog?
4. Where is the Crescent Hotel located?
5. What is the name of the most haunted hotel in Dallas, Texas?
6. Which hotel has probably been visited by more U.S. Presidents than any other hotel in America?
7. Lizzie Borden's father was struck with an ax forty-one times. True or false?
8. The Bullock Hotel is haunted by the ghost of Wild Bill Hickok. True or false?
9. What's the name of the ghost that haunts the Grove Park Inn?
10. Guests are not allowed to stay in Room 18 in the St. James Hotel because the resident ghost has been known to harm staff and guests by pushing them down, slapping them, and/or throwing them into the wall. True or False?

Quiz Answers:

1. John Belushi overdosed here and since that time there have been sightings and incidents in the bungalow where it happened; 2. *The Shining*; 3. Lemp Mansion Restaurant and Inn; 4. Ozark Mountains of Arkansas; 5. Adolphus Hotel; 6. Hotel del Coronado; 7. False. A popular rhyme says that "Lizzie Borden took an axe and gave her mother forty whacks. When she saw what she had done, she gave her father forty-one. But the truth is that her father suffered 11 blows; 8. False. Seth Bullock is believed to haunt the hotel; 9. Pink Lady; 10. True. The ghost obviously does not want anyone in this room so the owners thought it best to leave him alone!

TERRANCE ZEPKE
Series Reading Order
& Guide

Series List

Most Haunted Series

Terrance Talks Travel Series

Cheap Travel Series

Spookiest Series

Stop Talking Series

Carolinas for Kids Series

Ghosts of the Carolinas Series

Books & Guides for the Carolinas Series

& More Books by Terrance Zepke

≈

Introduction

Here is a list of titles by Terrance Zepke. They are presented in chronological order although they do not need to be read in any particular order.

Also included is an author bio, a personal message from Terrance, and some other information you may find helpful.

All books are available as digital and print books. They can be found on Amazon, Barnes and Noble, Kobo, Apple iBooks, GooglePlay, Smashwords, or through your favorite independent bookseller.

For more about this author and her books visit her Author Page at:

http://www.amazon.com/Terrance-Zepke/e/B000APJNIA/.

You can also connect with Terrance on Twitter **@terrancezepke** or on

www.facebook.com/terrancezepke

www.pinterest.com/terrancezepke

www.goodreads.com/terrancezepke

Sign up for weekly email notifications of the **Terrance Talks Travel** blog to be the first to learn about new episodes of her travel show, cheap travel tips, free downloadable TRAVEL REPORTS, and discover her TRIP PICK OF THE WEEK at www.terrancetalkstravel.com or sign up for her **Mostly Ghostly** blog at www.terrancezepke.com.

≈

You can follow her travel show, **TERRANCE TALKS TRAVEL: ÜBER ADVENTURES on** www.blogtalkradio.com/terrancetalkstravel or subscribe to it at **iTunes.**

Warning: Listening to this show could lead to a spectacular South African safari, hot-air ballooning over the Swiss Alps, Disney Adventures, and Tornado Tours!

≈

Terrance Zepke is co-host of the writing show, **A WRITER'S JOURNEY: FROM BLANK PAGE TO PUBLISHED.** All episodes can be found on **iTunes** or on www.terrancezepke.com.

≈

AUTHOR BIO

Terrance Zepke studied Journalism at the University of Tennessee and later received a Master's degree in Mass Communications from the University of South Carolina. She studied parapsychology at the renowned Rhine Research Center.

Zepke spends much of her time happily traveling around the world but always returns home to the Carolinas where she lives part-time in both states. She has written hundreds of articles and more than fifty books. She is the host of *Terrance Talks Travel: Über Adventures* and co-host of *A Writer's Journey: From Blank Page to Published*. Additionally, this award-winning and best-selling author has been featured in many publications and programs, such as NPR, CNN, *The Washington Post,* Associated Press, Travel with Rick Steves, Around the World, *Publishers Weekly,* World Travel & Dining with Pierre Wolfe, *San Francisco Chronicle*, Good Morning Show, *Detroit Free Press*, The Learning Channel, and The Travel Channel.

When she's not investigating haunted places, searching for pirate treasure, or climbing lighthouses, she is most likely packing for her next adventure to some far flung place, such as Reykjavik or Kwazulu Natal. Some of her favorite adventures include piranha fishing on the Amazon, shark cage diving in South Africa, hiking the Andes Mountains Inca Trail, camping in the Himalayas, dog-sledding in the Arctic Circle, and a gorilla safari in the Congo.

≈

MOST HAUNTED SERIES

A Ghost Hunter's Guide to the Most Haunted Places in America
(2012)
https://read.amazon.com/kp/embed?asin=B0085SG22O&previe
w=newtab&linkCode=kpe&ref_=cm_sw_r_kb_dp_zerQwb1AM
J0R4

A Ghost Hunter's Guide to the Most Haunted Houses in America
(2013)
https://read.amazon.com/kp/embed?asin=B00C3PUMGC&previ
ew=newtab&linkCode=kpe&ref_=cm_sw_r_kb_dp_BfrQwb1W
F1Y6T

*A Ghost Hunter's Guide to the Most Haunted Hotels & Inns in
America* (2014)
https://read.amazon.com/kp/embed?asin=B00C3PUMGC&previ
ew=newtab&linkCode=kpe

*A Ghost Hunter's Guide to the Most Haunted Historic Sites in
America* (2016)
https://www.amazon.com/Ghost-Hunters-Haunted-Historic-
America-
ebook/dp/B01LXADK90/ref=sr_1_1?s=books&ie=UTF8&qid=1
475973918&sr=1-
1&keywords=a+ghost+hunter%27s+guide+to+the+most+haunte
d+historic+sites+in+america

*The Ghost Hunter's MOST HAUNTED Box Set (3 in 1):
Discover America's Most Haunted Destinations* (2016)
https://read.amazon.com/kp/embed?asin=B01HISAAJM&previe
w=newtab&linkCode=kpe&ref_=cm_sw_r_kb_dp_ulz-
xbNKND7VT

MOST HAUNTED and SPOOKIEST Sampler Box Set: Featuring *A GHOST HUNTER'S GUIDE TO THE MOST HAUNTED PLACES IN AMERICA* and *SPOOKIEST CEMETERIES* (2017)

https://read.amazon.com/kp/embed?asin=B01N17EEOM&preview=newtab&linkCode=kpe&ref_=cm_sw_r_kb_dp_.JFLybCTN3QEF

≈

TERRANCE TALKS TRAVEL SERIES

Terrance Talks Travel: A Pocket Guide to South Africa (2015)
https://read.amazon.com/kp/embed?asin=B00PSTFTLI&preview
=newtab&linkCode=kpe&ref_=cm_sw_r_kb_dp_pirQwb12XZX
65

Terrance Talks Travel: A Pocket Guide to African Safaris (2015)
https://read.amazon.com/kp/embed?asin=B00PSTFZSA&previe
w=newtab&linkCode=kpe&ref_=cm_sw_r_kb_dp_jhrQwb0P8Z
87G

Terrance Talks Travel: A Pocket Guide to Adventure Travel
(2015)
https://read.amazon.com/kp/embed?asin=B00UKMAVQG&prev
iew=newtab&linkCode=kpe&ref_=cm_sw_r_kb_dp_ThrQwb1P
VVZAZ

*Terrance Talks Travel: A Pocket Guide to Florida Keys
(including Key West & The Everglades)* (2016)
http://www.amazon.com/Terrance-Talks-Travel-Including-
Everglades-
ebook/dp/B01EWHML58/ref=sr_1_1?s=books&ie=UTF8&qid=
1461897775&sr=1-
1&keywords=terrance+talks+travel%3A+a+pocket+guide+to+th
e+florida+keys

Terrance Talks Travel: The Quirky Tourist Guide to Key West
(2017)
https://www.amazon.com/Terrance-
Zepke/e/B000APJNIA/ref=sr_ntt_srch_lnk_1?qid=1485052308
&sr=8-1

Terrance Talks Travel: The Quirky Tourist Guide to Cape Town
(2017)
https://www.amazon.com/Terrance-

Zepke/e/B000APJNIA/ref=sr_ntt_srch_lnk_1?qid=1485052308&sr=8-1

Terrance Talks Travel: The Quirky Tourist Guide to Reykjavik (2017)
https://www.amazon.com/Terrance-Zepke/e/B000APJNIA/ref=sr_ntt_srch_lnk_15?qid=1488514258&sr=8-15

Terrance Talks Travel: The Quirky Tourist Guide to Charleston, South Carolina (2017)
https://www.amazon.com/Terrance-Zepke/e/B000APJNIA/ref=sr_ntt_srch_lnk_15?qid=1488514258&sr=8-15

Terrance Talks Travel: The Quirky Tourist Guide to Ushuaia (2017)
https://www.amazon.com/Terrance-Zepke/e/B000APJNIA/ref=sr_ntt_srch_lnk_15?qid=1488514258&sr=8-15

Terrance Talks Travel: The Quirky Tourist Guide to Antarctica (2017) https://www.amazon.com/Terrance-Zepke/e/B000APJNIA/ref=sr_ntt_srch_lnk_1?qid=1489092624&sr=8-1

TERRANCE TALKS TRAVEL: The Quirky Tourist Guide to Machu Picchu & Cuzco (Peru) 2017
https://read.amazon.com/kp/embed?asin=B07147HLQY&preview=newtab&linkCode=kpe&ref_=cm_sw_r_kb_dp_HmZmzb9FT5E0P

African Safari Box Set: Featuring TERRANCE TALKS TRAVEL: *A Pocket Guide to South Africa* and *TERRANCE TALKS TRAVEL: A Pocket Guide to African Safaris* (2017)

Terrance Zepke

https://read.amazon.com/kp/embed?asin=B01MUH6VJU&preview=newtab&linkCode=kpe&ref_=cm_sw_r_kb_dp_xLFLybAQKFA0B

≈

CHEAP TRAVEL SERIES

How to Cruise Cheap! (2017)

https://www.amazon.com/Cruise-Cheap-CHEAP-TRAVEL-Book-ebook/dp/B01N6NYM1N/

How to Fly Cheap! (2017)

https://www.amazon.com/How-Cheap-CHEAP-TRAVEL-Book-ebook/dp/B01N7Q81YG/

How to Travel Cheap! (2017)

https://read.amazon.com/kp/embed?asin=B01N7Q81YG&preview=newtab&linkCode=kpe&ref_=cm_sw_r_kb_dp_j78KybJVSCXDX

How to Travel FREE or Get Paid to Travel! (2017)

https://read.amazon.com/kp/embed?asin=B01N7Q81YG&preview=newtab&linkCode=kpe&ref_=cm_sw_r_kb_dp_j78KybJVSCXDX

CHEAP TRAVEL SERIES (4 IN 1) BOX SET (2017)

https://read.amazon.com/kp/embed?asin=B071ZGV1TY&preview=newtab&linkCode=kpe&ref_=cm_sw_r_kb_dp_rlZmzbSPV8KG9

Terrance Zepke

SPOOKIEST SERIES

Spookiest Lighthouses (2013)
https://read.amazon.com/kp/embed?asin=B00EAAQA2S&previe
w

Spookiest Battlefields (2015)
https://read.amazon.com/kp/embed?asin=B00XUSWS3G&previ
ew=newtab&linkCode=kpe&ref_=cm_sw_r_kb_dp_okrQwb0TR
9F8M

Spookiest Cemeteries (2016)
http://www.amazon.com/Terrance-
Zepke/e/B000APJNIA/ref=sr_ntt_srch_lnk_1?qid=1457641303
&sr=8-1

Spookiest Objects (2017)
https://read.amazon.com/kp/embed?asin=B0728FMVZF&previe
w=newtab&linkCode=kpe&ref_=cm_sw_r_kb_dp_eqZmzbN217
2VR

*Spookiest Box Set (3 in 1): Discover America's Most Haunted
Destinations* (2016)
https://read.amazon.com/kp/embed?asin=B01HH2OM4I&previe
w=newtab&linkCode=kpe&ref_=cm_sw_r_kb_dp_Anz-
xbT3SDEZS

MOST HAUNTED and SPOOKIEST Sampler Box Set: Featuring *A GHOST
HUNTER'S GUIDE TO THE MOST HAUNTED PLACES IN AMERICA* and
SPOOKIEST CEMETERIES (2017)

https://read.amazon.com/kp/embed?asin=B01N17EEOM&preview=n
ewtab&linkCode=kpe&ref_=cm_sw_r_kb_dp_.JFLybCTN3QEF

≈

STOP TALKING SERIES

Stop Talking & Start Writing Your Book (2015)
https://read.amazon.com/kp/embed?asin=B012YHTIAY&previe
w=newtab&linkCode=kpe&ref_=cm_sw_r_kb_dp_qlrQwb1N7G
3YF

Stop Talking & Start Publishing Your Book (2015)
https://read.amazon.com/kp/embed?asin=B013HHV1LE&previe
w=newtab&linkCode=kpe&ref_=cm_sw_r_kb_dp_WlrQwb1F6
3MFD

Stop Talking & Start Selling Your Book (2015)
https://read.amazon.com/kp/embed?asin=B015YAO33K&previe
w=newtab&linkCode=kpe&ref_=cm_sw_r_kb_dp_ZkrQwb188J
8BE

Stop Talking & Start Writing Your Book Series (3 in 1) Box Set
(2016) https://www.amazon.com/Stop-Talking-Start-Writing-
Box-
ebook/dp/B01M58J5AZ/ref=sr_1_5?s=books&ie=UTF8&qid=1
475974073&sr=1-5&keywords=stop+talking+and+start+writing

≈

Terrance Zepke

CAROLINAS FOR KIDS SERIES

Lighthouses of the Carolinas for Kids (2009)
http://www.amazon.com/Lighthouses-Carolinas-Kids-Terrance-Zepke/dp/1561644293/ref=asap_bc?ie=UTF8

Pirates of the Carolinas for Kids (2009)
https://read.amazon.com/kp/embed?asin=B01BJ3VSWK&preview=newtab&linkCode=kpe&ref_=cm_sw_r_kb_dp_rGrXwb0XDTSTA

Ghosts of the Carolinas for Kids (2011)
https://read.amazon.com/kp/embed?asin=B01BJ3VSVQ&preview=newtab&linkCode=kpe&ref_=cm_sw_r_kb_dp_XLrXwb0E7N1AK

≈

GHOSTS OF THE CAROLINAS SERIES

Ghosts of the Carolina Coasts (1999)
http://www.amazon.com/Ghosts-Carolina-Coasts-Terrance-Zepke/dp/1561641758/ref=asap_bc?ie=UTF8

The Best Ghost Tales of South Carolina (2004)
http://www.amazon.com/Best-Ghost-Tales-South-Carolina/dp/1561643068/ref=asap_bc?ie=UTF8

Ghosts & Legends of the Carolina Coasts (2005)
https://read.amazon.com/kp/embed?asin=B01AGQJABW&preview=newtab&linkCode=kpe&ref_=cm_sw_r_kb_dp_VKrXwb1Q09794

The Best Ghost Tales of North Carolina (2006)
https://read.amazon.com/kp/embed?asin=B01BJ3VSV6&preview=newtab&linkCode=kpe&ref_=cm_sw_r_kb_dp_6IrXwb0XKT90Q

≈

Terrance Zepke

BOOKS & GUIDES FOR THE CAROLINAS SERIES

Pirates of the Carolinas (2005)
http://www.amazon.com/Pirates-Carolinas-Terrance-Zepke/dp/1561643440/ref=asap_bc?ie=UTF8

Coastal South Carolina: Welcome to the Lowcountry (2006)
http://www.amazon.com/Coastal-South-Carolina-Welcome-Lowcountry/dp/1561643483/ref=asap_bc?ie=UTF8

Coastal North Carolina: Its Enchanting Islands, Towns & Communities (2011)
http://www.amazon.com/Coastal-North-Carolina-Terrance-Zepke/dp/1561645117/ref=asap_bc?ie=UTF8

Lighthouses of the Carolinas: A Short History & Guide (2011)
https://read.amazon.com/kp/embed?asin=B01AGQJA7G&preview=newtab&linkCode=kpe&ref_=cm_sw_r_kb_dp_UHrXwb09A22P1

≈

MORE BOOKS BY TERRANCE ZEPKE

Lowcountry Voodoo: Tales, Spells & Boo Hags (2009)
https://read.amazon.com/kp/embed?asin=B018WAGUC6&previ
ew=newtab&linkCode=kpe&ref_=cm_sw_r_kb_dp_UmrQwb19
AVSYG

Ghosts of Savannah (2012)
http://www.amazon.com/Ghosts-Savannah-Terrance-
Zepke/dp/1561645303/ref=asap_bc?ie=UTF8

How to Train Any Puppy or Dog Using Three Simple Strategies
(2017)
https://www.amazon.com/Train-Puppy-Using-Simple-Strategies-
ebook/dp/B01MZ5GN2M/ref=asap_bc?ie=UTF8

*Fiction books written under a pseudonym

≈

Message from the Author

The primary purpose of this guide is to introduce you to some titles you may not have known about. Another reason for it is to let you know all the ways you can connect with me. Authors love to hear from readers. We truly appreciate you more than you'll ever know. Please feel free to send me a comment or question via the comment form found on every page on www.terrancezepke.com and www.terrancetalkstravel.com or follow me on your favorite social media. Don't forget that you can also listen to my writing podcast on iTunes, **A Writer's Journey**, or my travel show, **Terrance Talks Travel: Über Adventures** on Blog Talk Radio and iTunes. The best way to make sure you don't miss any episodes of these shows (and find a complete archive of shows), new book releases and giveaways, contests, my TRIP PICK OF THE WEEK, cheap travel tips, free downloadable ghost and travel reports, and more is to subscribe to *Terrance Talks Travel* on www.terrancetalkstravel.com or *Mostly Ghostly* on www.terrancezepke.com. If you'd like to learn more about any of my books, you can find in-depth descriptions and "look inside" options through most online booksellers. Also, please note that links to book previews have been included in SERIES section of this booklet for your convenience.

Thank you for your interest and HAPPY READING!

Terrance

Turn the page for a special preview of the second book in Terrance Zepke's 'most haunted' series:

A GHOST HUNTER'S GUIDE TO THE MOST HAUNTED HOUSES IN AMERICA

Now available from Safari Publishing

Korner's Folly House

FUN FACTS:

The structure has been dubbed "The Strangest House in the World."

The house has been officially certified as "haunted" by as many as four ghosts.

The first private theater in America was inside this house. The theater, Cupid's Park, still exists.

The History

The Strangest House in the World. That's what it was once called by an architectural magazine, *Preservation*, and the name stuck. It's no wonder it's considered such a strange dwelling. It is a three-story house that has seven levels. The 6,000-square foot Victorian mansion has twenty-two rooms with ceiling heights ranging from six feet to twenty-five feet. There are many unusual murals and artwork in the house, as well as a unique air distribution system. Another unusual feature is the smoking room. Accidental fires posed a serious threat in those days. With that in mind, a fireproof room was built onto the house. This is the only place that smoking was permitted within the house. No two doorways are the same. The same is true for the fifteen fireplaces. There are numerous cubbyholes and trapdoors throughout the odd house.

The house was the architectural vision of one man, Jule Gilmer Korner. He began building the house in 1878. Two years later, he moved in but continued to make changes to the house for many years. It was built to showcase his interior design business, but later it became a home for his family.

He hired a freed slave to run his household. She affectionately became known as 'Aunt Dealy.' She took good care of the house and Jule until he got married in 1886. After that, the job fell to his new wife, Polly Alice Masten Korner. A cottage was built behind the house and Aunt Dealy moved out of the main house and into this outbuilding.

Jule and Polly had two children. Child-sized rooms were constructed to accommodate them. Many other changes were made, such as the additions of a ladies sitting room and a library. The top story of the house was made into a children's theatre, Cupid's Park. Puppet shows, plays, and recitals were held here for all the children in town to enjoy. Theatrical productions are still produced here on occasion. Underneath the theatre is a huge room that is known as the Reception Room. This is where Jule and Polly did most of their entertaining.

Cupid's Park Theatre (top floor of house)

Because of its odd design and never-ending renovations, a visiting cousin once remarked that "This will surely be Jule Korner's folly." Instead of being offended, Jule was amused. He promptly had a plaque made that read "Korner's Folly" and hung it outside the front door.

Jule Korner died in 1924. Right up to his death he was still working on the house because he never felt that it was finished. Polly died ten years later. The property stayed in the family until the 1970s when it was turned over to the non-profit group, Korner's Folly Foundation.

The Hauntings

Korner's Folly has been investigated by several ghost groups and certified as officially haunted. I have spent the night inside the house, along with an investigative team from the Winston-Salem Paranormal Society. We hunkered down for the night in various rooms across the house, which were reportedly the most haunted areas. These included the Reception Room, Cupid's Park, the ladies sitting room, and one of the bedrooms.

The most haunted area of the house is believed to be the Reception Room, so this is where I chose to be. The psychic and a lead investigator were also in the room with me. The bulk of the monitoring equipment was set up here, so we could see what was going on in other parts of the house. The director of the foundation, Bruce Frankel, had given us a private tour and implicit instructions regarding our overnight stay. One of the rules was not to touch the furniture, so the three of us were seated in folding chairs in the middle of the room. Beside me was the "kissing couch." It has an "S" shape so that the man and woman can sit on opposite sides and face one another to talk or steal a kiss.

At one point in the evening, I suddenly felt very cold and got a weird sensation. As I was trying to figure this out given that it was a hot June night, I felt something on my arm. Startled, I soon realized that it was the hand of the psychic, who was seated next to me. He spoke softly, "I thought you should know that I sense a female presence on the kissing couch." I quickly processed what he was saying. A ghost was beside me!

She moved around the room, standing next to the piano and near the doorway before she disappeared. I knew when she had moved away from me because the cold (and weird) feeling disappeared as suddenly as it had occurred.

We had some questionable EVPs and one of the team members felt a pinch on her behind when no one was standing near her. That was believed to be the spirit of Jule, who had a reputation as a "ladies man" before he got married. He has been known to pinch female visitors on the behind sometimes during their tours.

Another group, Southern Paranormal and Anomaly Research Society (SPARS), certified the house as being "officially haunted" at the conclusion of their investigation. They picked up lots of EVPs of moaning and "peek-a-boo," which was a favorite game of the Korner children. The group also saw unexplainable shadows and orbs on their images.

If all the reports are true, then Korner's Folly is haunted by several spirits. These include Jule Korner, his kids, and Aunt Dealy and/or Polly Korner.

Wide angle view of the haunted ballroom and kissing couch

Visitor Information

The house is open to the public for daytime tours. Also, special events are held throughout the year. The biggest and best is its Holiday Open House. During December, the house is decorated to the hilt, usually by professional interior designers. Take it from me, the house looks properly festive. Jule Korner would be proud!

413 S. Main Street

Kernersville, NC 27284

www.kornersfolly.org

Kernersville is 2.5 hours from Asheville, NC (155 miles); 7 hours from Columbus, OH (390 miles); and 10.5 hours from Memphis, TN (650 miles).

Index

A

B

C

D

H

J

Jim Carrey. *See Stanley Hotel*
John Adam Lemp, 100
John Belushi, 55, 56, 58, 154. *See Chateau Marmont*
John Morse, 41, 42
Jule Korner, 161

K

Kate Morgan. *See Hotel del Coronado*
Kernersville, NC, 165
Korner's Folly House, 158

L

Lavender Lady. *See Lillian Lemp*
Lemp Mansion Restaurant & Inn, 6, 98, 99
Lemp Western Brewing Co., 100
Leone Johnson, 151
Lillian Lemp, 104
Little Imp. *See St. James Hotel*
Lizbeth. *See Lizzie Borden*
Lizzie Borden, 6, 37, 38, 40, 43, 50, 51, 153, 154
Lizzie Borden Bed and Breakfast Museum, 51
Lizzie Borden House B & B, 37, 38
Long Hot Summer

See St. James Hotelht.
Seth Bullock, 133, 134, 135, 137, 154
Siege of Charleston, 65
South Carolina, 3, 6, 8, 66, 68, 155, 156
St. Francisville, LA, 36
St. James Hotel, 6, 9, 74, 76, 80, 153
St. Louis, Missouri, 106
Stanley Hotel, 6, 8, 10, 11, 13, 14, 15, 17
Stanley Steamer, 13
Stephen King, 8, 15, 17, 21
Sunset Boulevard, 59

T

TAPS
   The Atlantic Paranormal Society, 105
The Grand Old Lady of the Ozarks. *See Crescent Hotel*
The Myrtles. See Myrtles Plantation
The Shining Ball'. *See Stanley Hotel*
Tombstone, 76
Torso Ghost. *See Battery Carriage House Inn*

W

Whiskey Rebellion, 28
Wild Bill Hickok. See Bullock Hotel
William J. Lemp, 99

Made in the USA
Columbia, SC
23 June 2020